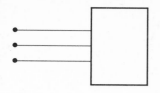

OMBUDSMEN IN THE
PUBLIC SECTOR

LAW AND POLITICAL CHANGE

Series Editors: Professor Cosmo Graham, Law School, University of Hull, and Professor Norman Lewis, Centre for Socio-Legal Studies, University of Sheffield.

Current titles:

Scott Davidson: *Human Rights*
Norman Lewis and Patrick Birkinshaw: *When Citizens Complain*
Michael Moran and Bruce Wood: *States, Regulation and the Medical Profession*
Mary Seneviratne: *Ombudsmen in the Public Sector*

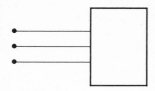

OMBUDSMEN IN THE PUBLIC SECTOR

Mary Seneviratne

OPEN UNIVERSITY PRESS
Buckingham • Philadelphia

Open University Press
Celtic Court
22 Ballmoor
Buckingham
MK18 1XW

and
1900 Frost Road, Suite 101
Bristol, PA 19007, USA

First Published 1994

A catalogue record of this book is available from the British Library

ISBN 0 335 15773 4 (hb)

Library of Congress Cataloging-in-Publication Data

Seneviratne, Mary, 1948–
    Ombudsmen in the public sector / Mary Seneviratne.
        p.   cm. — (Law and political change)
    Includes bibliographical references and index.
    ISBN 0-335-15773-4 (HB)
    1. Ombudsman — Great Britain.   I. Title.   II. Series.
JN329.043S46   1994
354.41009′1 — dc20   93-28577
                                                           CIP

Typeset by Colset Private Limited, Singapore
Printed in Great Britain by St Edmundsbury Press, Bury St Edmunds, Suffolk

To Anna, Sarah and Christopher

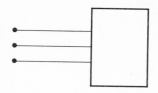

CONTENTS

Preface and acknowledgements   viii
List of cases   x
List of statutes   xi

1   INTRODUCTION   1

2   THE PARLIAMENTARY COMMISSIONER   17
    FOR ADMINISTRATION

3   THE HEALTH SERVICE COMMISSIONER   59

4   THE LOCAL GOVERNMENT OMBUDSMEN   83

5   CONCLUSION   121

Appendix 1   Government Departments and Other Bodies   134
             Subject to Investigation by the Parliamentary
             Commissioner for Administration
Appendix 2   Addresses of the Public Sector Ombudsmen   138
Bibliography   140
Index   146

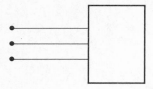

PREFACE AND ACKNOWLEDGEMENTS

The growth of ombudsmen in both the public and private sectors has been a feature of modern life. Although they originated in Sweden at the beginning of the nineteenth century, interest in ombudsmen in the UK is normally associated with a 1961 report by Justice, *The Citizen and the Administration*. That report resulted in the setting up of the office of the Parliamentary Commissioner for Administration in 1967. Since then, the public sector has acquired ombudsmen for local government and the health service.

Writing soon after the introduction of the Parliamentary ombudsman, Gregory and Hutchesson (1975), in their major study of that office, noted:

> Even now, more than six years after the establishment of the Office, the functions of the Parliamentary Commissioner are certainly not as well understood as they might be, and there is still a good deal of uncertainty about when and how he can assist Members of Parliament and their constituents.

Sadly, some twenty-five years after the establishment of the office, the position seems to be the same, with widespread ignorance of all the public sector, or classical, ombudsmen, and few readily accessible sources of information about their work. This book is intended to dispel some of this ignorance.

My interest in ombudsmen began some years ago when I was involved in a research project which examined local authority complaints procedures.

Such a project necessarily involved an examination of the role of the Local Government Ombudsmen. Rather than confine this book to a discussion of the work of the Local Government Ombudsmen, I decided that it would be more useful to include the other ombudsmen in the public sector. The purpose of the book, therefore, is to describe and evaluate these ombudsmen, but its scope is restricted to the ombudsmen in England. It will thus deal with the Parliamentary Commissioner for Administration, the Health Service Commissioner and the Commissioners for Local Administration in England.

It is not a theoretical work. Nevertheless, it is hoped that the book will be of interest to those studying public law, as well as those studying public administration, social work, social policy and politics. Although it is not intended as a handbook, it should provide useful information for those involved in dealing with complaints by citizens about the public services. In this respect, the legal profession has an important part to play. Justice, in its 1988 review *Administrative Justice: Some Necessary Reforms*, spoke about the special responsibility of members of the legal profession to be well informed about the assistance that an ombudsman may be able to give to their clients. In addition, Justice called upon those responsible for legal education to ensure that administrative law courses include instruction on the ombudsmen.

On a personal note, I would like to express my thanks to a number of people for their help and support during the writing of this book. I am especially grateful to Norman Lewis for encouraging my interest in the area some years ago, and for suggesting that I write this book. My thanks also go to William Reid and Gordon Adams for their helpful comments, and to David Nice and Richard Oswald for their very useful comments on some of the draft chapters. Diane Longley and Rhoda James not only commented on drafts, but also offered help and encouragement, for which I am grateful. Above all, I wish to thank my family: Ian Brownlee for his love and support; Anna and Sarah for their patience and understanding; and Christopher, its newest member, for sleeping just long enough during the first few weeks of his life to enable me to finish this book on time.

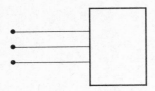

LIST OF CASES

Council of Civil Service Unions v. *Minister for the Civil Service (GCHQ case)* [1985] AC 374   9

R v. *Commissioner for Local Administration in England: ex parte Newman and another* CA (unreported)   94–5

R v. *Local Commissioner for Administration: ex parte Bradford Metropolitan City Council* [1979] QBD 278; [1979] 2 All ER 881   7–8, 86, 102

R v. *Local Commissioner for Administration: ex parte Croydon LBC* [1989] 1 All ER 1033   106

R v. *Local Commissioner for Administration: ex parte Eastleigh Borough Council* [1988] QBD 855; [1988] 3 All ER 151   8, 86, 106

R v. *London Borough of Enfield: ex parte T.F.Unwin (Roydon) Ltd* (1989) 46 Build LR 1   89

R v. *Parliamentary Commissioner for Administration: ex parte Lithgow and another* (1990) (unreported)   27

R v. *Secretary of State for Foreign and Commonwealth Affairs: ex parte Everett* (1987) *The Independent* 4 December 1987   22

Re: A complaint against Liverpool City Council [1977] 2 All ER 650   103

Re Fletcher [1970] 2 All ER 527   26

Roy v. *Kensington and Chelsea and Westminster Family Practitioner Committee* (1990) 1 Med LR 328   65

Roy v. *Kensington and Chelsea and Westminster Family Practitioner Committee* [1992] 1 AC 624   65

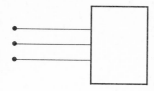

LIST OF STATUTES

Broadcasting Act 1990   42
Building Societies Act 1986   4
Children Act 1989   107
Commissioner for Complaints (Northern Ireland) Act 1969   84, 99
Community Care Act 1990   107
Courts and Legal Services Act 1990   22
Education Act 1980   93
Education Reform Act 1988   92–3
Exchequer and Audit Act 1866   18
Extradition Act 1870   22
Fugitive Offenders Act 1881   22
Hospital Complaints Procedure Act 1985   61, 62, 78
Local Government Act 1974   4, 84, 86, 95, 109, 117
Local Government Act 1978   98
Local Government Act 1988   89, 101, 109, 115
Local Government and Housing Act 1989   101, 114, 116–17, 118
Local Government Finance Act 1982   98, 112
Local Government and Planning Act 1980   103
Local Government, Planning and Land Act 1980   114
Local Government (Scotland) Act 1975   84
National Health Service Act 1946   65
National Health Service Act 1977   60, 65, 70
National Health Service and Community Care Act 1990   61, 65

National Health Service Reorganisation Act 1973   **4, 23, 60**
Parliamentary and Health Service Commissioners Act 1987   **19, 21, 71–2, 75**
Parliamentary Commissioner Act 1967   **4, 17, 19, 20, 21, 60, 122**
Parliamentary Commissioner (Consular Complaints) Act 1981   **21**
Police Act 1976   **21**
Police and Criminal Evidence Act 1984   **25**
Prevention of Fraud (Investments) Act 1958   **34**

INTRODUCTION

This book describes and evaluates the work of the ombudsmen in the public sector. These ombudsmen, created by statute, act as independent complaints handlers for disputes involving citizens and the administration. In the United Kingdom there are seven people who fit this description. First, there is the Parliamentary Commissioner for Administration (PCA), who is also the Health Service Commissioner (HSC). In Northern Ireland there is the Northern Ireland Parliamentary Commissioner for Administration, who is also the Commissioner for Complaints. There are five Commissioners for Local Administration: three for England, one for Wales and one for Scotland. This book will concentrate on the Parliamentary Commissioner for Administration, the Health Service Commissioner and the Commissioners for Local Administration in England. It will not deal with Northern Ireland, nor with the Scottish and Welsh Local Commissioners. In some respects the Police Complaints Authority may properly be seen as an ombudsman system, but its remit is highly specialized, and it will not be discussed in this work. The recently created Prisons Ombudsman, who is not a statutory ombudsman, will be discussed within the context of the PCA.

One reason for my writing this book is that, although the first public sector ombudsman came into existence twenty-five years ago, the functions of these ombudsmen are not generally well understood. There are few readily accessible sources of information about their work. There is confusion and uncertainty about their role and, with the introduction of ombudsmen in the private sector, this confusion could be exacerbated. It is hoped that this book will clarify some of these issues, and will indicate how users of the services which the ombudsmen have to offer can utilize them to their best advantage.

The origins of each of the ombudsmen will be looked at individually within the ensuing chapters, but this chapter will look generally at the reasons for, and use of, ombudsmen.

THE DEVELOPMENT OF OMBUDSMEN

The idea that citizens should be entitled to complain against specific acts of their rulers, and that their complaints should be independently investigated, goes back thousands of years (see Bell and Vaughan 1988). However, the establishment of a specific office to investigate citizen complaints against public officials is relatively recent, having started in Sweden in the early nineteenth century. Indeed the word 'ombudsman' was originally a Swedish word, meaning a representative or agent of the people or a group of people. In relation to the public sector, the word is now used generally to refer to an officer appointed by the legislature to handle complaints against administrative and judicial action.

The institution of the *Justitieombudsman* was created in Sweden in 1809, and was given the task of prosecuting culpable administrators and judges. Now the Swedish ombudsman ensures that those who hold public office respect the law and properly fulfil their obligations. She or he is appointed by the legislature to handle complaints against administrative and judicial action.

Over one hundred years passed before the idea was taken up elsewhere, and then it remained for many years within Scandinavia. In 1919, Finland became the second country to create an ombudsman, when provision was made in the constitution for a Parliamentary ombudsman and a Chancellor. The Chancellor's role was to see that the authorities and officials complied with the law and performed their duties, 'so that no person shall suffer injuries to his rights' (Article 46). The ombudsman was to supervise 'observance of the law in the proceedings of courts and other authorities' (Article 49).

Finland was followed by Denmark in 1955, when the Folketingets ombudsman, or Parliamentary Commissioner, took office and began to function. The Danish ombudsman supervises civil and military central government administration, apart from the courts. Jurisdiction covers ministers and civil servants and all other persons acting in the service of the state, except those engaged in judicial administration. In 1962 the jurisdiction was widened to include local officials when they acted in matters for which recourse could be had to a central government authority, although local government in general was outside jurisdiction. Although the ombudsman can comment on the quality of administration there is no power to change decisions, so he or she cannot overturn the results of poor administration.

The introduction of the Danish ombudsman marked the beginning of a worldwide interest in ombudsmen. In 1963, Norway set up a Parliamentary ombudsman for civil administration, the Stortingets ombudsman, using the Danish ombudsman as a model. The Danish ombudsman was also the model for the New Zealand ombudsman, which was created in 1962, New Zealand being the first country outside Scandinavia to set up such a scheme. The introduction of an ombudsman in a common law country sparked off a great deal of the interest in ombudsmen throughout the world.

Although the idea of ombudsmen originated almost two hundred years ago, its modern equivalents have been adapted to suit local conditions. The institutions themselves, and their operating methods and objectives, vary from country to country, which is not surprising given their different constitutional positions. In the Scandinavian countries, the ombudsman plays a more significant role than in the United Kingdom, since they do not have a Westminster style government, and most of the administration is conducted through agencies rather than through government departments.

By the 1970s ombudsmen had appeared in many parts of the world, and by 1983 the ombudsman idea had been accepted by almost every country in Western Europe. In the past twenty years there has been an extraordinary spread of ombudsmen systems across the world, the major exception being the United States of America. Ombudsmen now operate in over forty countries on a national, state, regional or municipal level (Haller 1988: 32). The popularity of the institution can be seen from its expansion from the public sector into the private sector.

Given this present worldwide interest in the ombudsman idea, it is strange that the system was not taken up by any country outside Scandinavia until after the Second World War. Rowat (1985) believes that the reason for the interest after the war was the expansion of state activity during and after the war, coupled with a new concern for protecting human rights and with the growth of public education and participation. It was these social conditions, together with the activities of the International Commission of Jurists and the United Nations, which favoured the interest in ombudsmen (Rowat 1985: 131).

Ombudsmen came to be seen as useful in helping to meet the problem of an expanded bureaucracy in the modern welfare state (Rowat 1985: 3), the activities of which had grown in range and complexity. The increase in the powers of discretion given to the executive side of government led to a need for additional protection against administrative arbitrariness,

particularly as there was often no redress for those aggrieved by administrative decisions (p. 49).

The growth of ombudsmen in both the public and private sectors has been
a feature of modern life. In this country, ombudsmen were introduced in the
public sector in the 1960s and 1970s, with the Parliamentary Commissioner
Act 1967, the National Health Service Reorganisation Act 1973 and the
Local Government Act 1974. More recently, ombudsmen have been introduced in the private sector. In 1981, the insurance industry created the
Insurance Ombudsman Bureau. This was followed in 1986 by the banks,
which established the Office of the Banking Ombudsman. The Building
Societies Act 1986 provided for an ombudsman scheme for that industry,
and the use of ombudsmen has now been extended to legal services,
pensions, estate agents and investments.

More recently, the Maastricht Treaty has provided for the establishment
of a European Community ombudsman to provide recourse to citizens
against maladministration in the activities of Community institutions
(Treaty on European Union 1992, Article 107d). The European Parliament
has also passed a Resolution to this effect (OJ C21/141, 25 January 1993).
The European Ombudsman is to be appointed by the European Parliament,
and will hold the same rank as a judge in the European Court of Justice.
Any natural or legal person residing or having a registered office in a member
state may make a complaint, either directly or through a Member of the
European Parliament. In addition, the ombudsman will be able to act on
his or her own initiative. The ombudsman will be able to investigate complaints of maladministration in the activities of Community institutions
or bodies, except the Court of Justice and the Court of First Instance acting
in their judicial role. Those investigated will be obliged to supply the
ombudsman with the information requested, and cannot refuse on the
grounds of confidentiality. The ombudsman will report to the European
Parliament.

There have also been calls for a Community Ombudsman for the private
sector to advise on transfrontier disputes within the European Community.
Such an ombudsman would also identify when jurisdiction should be with
the European Courts and when at national level. Where appropriate, the
ombudsman could act as an arbitrator, investigating cases and informing
consumers and their associations how to obtain redress (ECG Briefing Paper
1990: 8).

WHAT IS AN OMBUDSMAN?

The proliferation of ombudsmen in the public and private sector has focused
attention on the essential characteristics of an ombudsman. While there are

'significantly different interpretations of what exactly the Ombudsman's functions are in separate systems' (Friedmann 1988: 107), and a number of problems of comparison, some definitions may be useful.

Although there are considerable differences according to national background, their common features were recognized some years ago by the International Bar Association, when it resolved in 1974 that an ombudsman was:

> An office provided for by the constitution or by an action of the legislature or parliament and headed by an independent, high-level public official who is responsible to the legislature or parliament, who receives complaints from aggrieved persons against government agencies, officials, and employees or who acts on his own motion, and who has the power to investigate, recommend corrective action, and issue reports.
>
> (Quoted in Haller 1988: 40)

Hill (1976: 12) provides another definition, which includes the fact that the office can use its 'extensive powers of investigation in performing a post-decision administrative audit' and that the findings are reported publicly, but that it cannot change administrative decisions. Ombudsmen constitute the subjects of interest for the International Ombudsman Institute at Alberta, Canada, and the European Ombudsman Institute at Innsbruck.

It is difficult to make worldwide comparisons, as these may depend upon the extent to which procedures exist for the resolution of disputes before a formal complaint is made. In a well-established ombudsman system, the ombudsman is at the top of a pyramid of grievance resolving machinery, and is the last port of call when other procedures are exhausted. Indeed, a significant development, alongside the creation of ombudsman institutions, is the introduction of 'in-house' dispute resolution procedures (Moore 1991: 7–8). However, worldwide, ombudsmen have two distinguishing features: constitutional independence and extensive powers of investigation (Moore 1991: 1–2).

The term 'ombudsman' is not used in the statutory title of any of the public sector ombudsmen in the United Kingdom. However, it is a term that is readily understood, and it is used for schemes in the private sector. At a recent conference for ombudsmen in the United Kingdom (Meriden 1991), the characteristics of the public sector, sometimes referred to as 'classical', ombudsman were discussed. It was accepted that it was 'an office created by statute, reporting to the legislature, with tenure, accessible to the citizen, with powers of discovery, protected by privilege, and with powers to investigate and make recommendations' (Hayes 1991: 5).

Of particular concern in the United Kingdom is how far the ombudsmen in the private sector display the necessary characteristics of an ombudsman, and whether the existence of ombudsmen beyond the public sector represents a strengthening or a dilution of the concept. In New Zealand a law was passed restricting the use of the title to the Parliamentary ombudsman (Hayes 1991: 5). There are no such restrictions in the UK, although the Local Government Ombudsman has discouraged the use of the word 'ombudsman' to describe an officer of a local authority responsible for investigating complaints, believing that the title should be reserved for use by ombudsmen who are independent of the organization against which a complaint is made (Commission for Local Administration *Annual Report* 1991–2: 44).

It is thought that ombudsmen in the private sphere should have as many as possible of the characteristics of the classical ombudsmen. That is, they should be created by statute and be independent of the body investigated, and there should be ease of access for complainants. They should have powers to investigate, the ability to make recommendations and the moral if not the legal authority to secure redress. Without these characteristics, the ombudsman becomes at best an institutional troubleshooter and at worst an extension of the normal public relations activity of an organization (Hayes 1991: 6).

Following on from the United Kingdom Ombudsman conference (Meriden 1991), a working party was set up to agree criteria for the use of the term 'ombudsman'. The working party consisted of five members: the Secretary of the Commission for Local Administration, the Scottish Local Ombudsman, the Director of the National Consumer Council, an academic and the Banking Ombudsman, who chaired the group. Four key criteria were identified by the working party: independence from those investigated, effectiveness, fairness and public accountability. The ombudsman should be accessible, the right to complain should be adequately publicized and those complaining should be able to do so free of charge. There should be a reasonable expectation that the decisions of the ombudsman will be complied with, and where they are not the ombudsman should have the power to publicize this at the expense of those investigated. As for accountability, an ombudsman should publish an annual report, and be entitled to publish anonymized reports of investigations.

It was also suggested by the working party that an association be set up and a UK Ombudsman Association has now been formed, chaired by the Banking Ombudsman. Its members include public and private sector ombudsmen from England, Scotland, Wales and Northern Ireland. The association was set up because, as the number of ombudsmen has grown rapidly in recent years, it was thought that it was time to establish a professional association with objects to which all recognized ombudsmen were committed. The association will formulate and promote standards to be met by recognized ombudsmen, and will define and publish criteria for the use of the term 'ombudsman'. Full membership of the association will be restricted to those who meet the criteria. This association has no statutory authority, and is purely a voluntary undertaking. There is no obligation to become a member of the association, and there is nothing in law to prevent those who are not members of the association from using the term 'ombudsman'. The voluntary nature of these initiatives is noteworthy. The government has neither instigated nor been involved with any of these developments.

OMBUDSMEN IN BRITAIN

The emergence of ombudsmen in the public sector in Britain was a result of a growing awareness within government of public disquiet over the ability of the institutions of central and local government to handle and respond to complaints about their activities in a fair and reasonable manner (see Birkinshaw 1985: 127). Britain's interest in the ombudsman concept is normally associated with the Whyatt Report (Justice 1961), which inquired into the arrangements that existed for redressing grievances and remedying maladministration.

The Whyatt Report resulted in the setting up of the office of the PCA. This office differed from the Scandinavian model of ombudsmen, as it was seen as an adjunct to Parliament as opposed to an agency independent of the political and administrative regimes (see Birkinshaw 1985: 129). The Whyatt Report itself had recommended that a distinction should be drawn between complaints about the merits of decisions, and complaints about bad administration, and this distinction has resulted in all the public sector ombudsmen having a restricted remit.

The public sector ombudsmen are concerned with examining grievances from citizens who have complaints against public authorities, that is, central government departments, local authorities and the health service. These complaints are essentially that injustice has been caused as a result of maladministration by the authority concerned. Complaints about the merits of decisions, or policy matters, cannot be investigated by the ombudsmen, although the HSC can investigate failures of service. Maladministration was not defined in any of the statutes that set up the ombudsmen, although during the debate on the Bill which established the PCA, maladministration was referred to in terms of 'bias, neglect, inattention, delay, incompetence, ineptitude, perversity, turpitude, arbitrariness and so on'.

Its meaning is imprecise, and ombudsmen have therefore had some flexibility in deciding what actions or inactions will constitute maladministration. The courts have had cause to examine its meaning in cases involving the Local Government Ombudsman. In *R* v. *Commissioners for Local*

Administration: ex parte Bradford MBC [1979] QB 287, Eveleigh J said that maladministration meant 'faulty administration', and May J in the High Court talked about 'bad administration'. In *R* v. *Commissioners for Local Administration: ex parte Eastleigh BC* [1980] QB 855, Lord Donaldson MR said that administration and maladministration in the context of the work of a local authority was concerned with the *manner* in which decisions by the authority were reached and the *manner* in which they were or were not implemented, adding that administration had nothing to do with the nature, quality or reasonableness of the decision itself.

This approach can be compared to that in New Zealand, where the ombudsman is not restricted to cases of maladministration, but is empowered to report on any decision, recommendation, act or omission which appears to have been contrary to law; is unreasonable, unjust, oppressive or improperly discriminatory; is based wholly or partly on a mistake of law or fact; or is wrong. In Denmark the ombudsman can criticize mistakes and unreasonable decisions, in a way that allows considerable latitude. In Norway the ombudsman looks at injustice, and can look at discretionary decisions which are clearly unreasonable or otherwise in conflict with fair administrative practice.

Issues in relation to maladministration will be taken up in subsequent chapters, but what is important to note here is that ombudsmen cannot be used as an appeal mechanism against administrative decisions. Even where there is a finding of maladministration in the way a decision has been made, the remedy is for a fresh decision to be made in a manner which does not involve maladministration.

GRIEVANCE RESOLUTION

Ombudsmen should be seen as one among many methods available for securing administrative justice. They are a method of grievance resolution. Until recently there was little theoretical or empirical work in relation to grievance redress outside of the courts, but interest in this area has increased over the past few years (see Rawlings 1986b for a review) and a 'complaints industry' seems to be emerging (see Crawford 1988: 246). In order to understand the place of ombudsmen in relation to the resolution of grievances, it is necessary to look briefly at the traditional methods of resolving grievances about public administration.

The traditional institution for the resolution of grievances is the courts, and in the past the courts have been seen as the protectors of rights. This is true for grievances of individuals against the state, as well as individuals in relation to each other. Legal remedies against the state include actions in contract and tort, as well as various statutory provisions for appeal by those aggrieved by the decisions of public authorities in specific cases. In addition, the decisions of public authorities are subject to judicial review.

However, the traditional legal methods of grievance resolution are beyond the reach of most citizens. The main problem with resorting to the courts is the cost, actual or potential, of advice and proceedings. Legal Aid, being means tested, can be claimed by very few people, and it depends upon people knowing their rights, knowing where to go for assistance, having a low income and coming within the eligibility criteria. Indeed, the problems of obtaining Legal Aid are probably worsening, and bodies such as the National Consumer Council and the Law Society have expressed concern about the decline in the number of people eligible (ECG Briefing Paper 1990: 8).

When delay and formality are added to the problem of cost, it is hardly surprising that alternative dispute resolution mechanisms have been introduced for dealing with disputes. For general consumer matters, these alternatives include conciliation and arbitration for small claims, which is a less costly procedure, and more easily accessible to consumers. Some industries, adopting a self-regulatory approach, have introduced codes of good practice on a voluntary basis. In the courts themselves there is a simplified small claims procedure for civil cases, which is less formal, less expensive and quicker.

As far as grievances in relation to administrative action are concerned, there is some overlap between the jurisdiction of the ombudsman and the powers of the courts in relation to judicial review. For example, the courts can look at illegality, irrationality and procedural impropriety in decision making (see *Council of Civil Service Unions* v. *Minister for the Civil Service* (GCHQ case) [1985] AC 374). The courts cannot attack decisions with which they may disagree on the merits, as the challenge on the basis of irrationality refers to a decision 'which is so outrageous in its defiance of logic or of accepted moral standards that no sensible person who had applied his mind to the question to be decided could have arrived at it' (GCHQ case, *per* Lord Diplock: 410).

If there is a successful challenge by way of judicial review, the decision of the public body concerned is quashed, or the decision is declared unlawful and of no effect, or, if the case involves a failure to perform a public duty, the public body can be ordered to perform its duty. However, the courts are not as flexible as the ombudsman and are not always an effective instrument for remedying wrongs in this area. In addition to being costly, cumbersome and slow, they have limited powers of review, being mainly concerned with the legality of decisions. For many minor matters, administrative review can be too burdensome an undertaking. However, judicial review can be a useful remedy, and the ombudsman and judicial review should be seen as complementary to each other (see Justice 1988: 86).

As an alternative dispute resolution mechanism, the ombudsman has a number of advantages over the courts. The courts operate on an adversarial model of grievance redress, but this has limitations as a method of righting wrongs in administration. The ombudsman uses inquisitorial methods, often operating informally, and his or her investigations do not impede the normal processes of government. The investigation powers given to the ombudsmen can often bring to light cases of bureaucratic maladministration that would otherwise pass unnoticed. On the other hand, there may be a finding that the complaint is without merit, in which case the fact that there has been an impartial and independent investigation may well serve to enhance morale in the public authority investigated.

The ombudsman is impartial, but has a conciliatory approach. It is not the aim of the investigation to antagonize public officials 'but to induce them to internalise fairness and justice values and to accept them as values that legitimately compete with effectiveness and other bureaucratic values for balanced accommodation' (Friedmann 1988: 114). In order to be effective, the ombudsman depends to a considerable extent on voluntary compliance from public officials, so cooperation has to be the norm. The ombudsman can also help to negotiate adjustments to decisions that are not illegal or otherwise subject to criticism, and 'suggest minor adjustments that overcome bureaucratic rigidity' (Gellhorn 1967: 433). However, there is no general review of discretion, and criticism is only appropriate where discretion is exercised for insupportable reasons.

The decisions of public authorities have increasingly been subjected to appeal in tribunals, rather than in the courts, but these administrative appeal bodies only cover a small portion of the total field of administrative action. Those which do exist have, on the whole, been very successful, but there is no general administrative appeals tribunal, so that a citizen must depend upon an individual statute conceding a right of appeal. There is no general duty imposed upon public administration to produce a grievance system of any sort that could be used by someone to register a complaint.

Elected representatives play an important part in individual grievance resolution. There is a long-established tradition of citizens using MPs when they wish to complain about the actions of central government departments and local government. Indeed the workload of MPs as a whole in relation to grievance handling is considerable: they receive, in total, an estimated 300,000 complaints a year, and write about 50,000 letters to ministers on behalf of constituents each year (see Gregory and Pearson 1992: 474). While I do not underestimate the important work MPs do in relation to grievance handling, they are restricted by time and expertise, and they do not have access to civil servants and departmental files. These problems are even more acute for local councillors. Being part-time and unpaid, councillors cannot be expected to devote more than a small part of their time to following up grievances of constituents. Ombudsmen can act as an aid to the work of elected members, and because of their wide investigative powers can achieve a resolution where MPs and councillors would be powerless.

Other methods of grievance resolution involve the political process. The classical remedy for maladministration in Britain is the individual responsibility of the minister to Parliament. However, it would clearly be impractical for ministers to resign every time mistakes were made in a department. Parliament itself is preoccupied with legislation and national and international policy. It cannot devote its collective time to individual grievances (see Clothier 1986: 205). The executive is unwilling to investigate itself, and the machinery for controlling it is inadequate. As long ago as 1968, Rowat recognized that the effectiveness of the Parliamentary question and of the adjournment debate was diminishing, as the field of administrative law was broadening (p. 269). Select committees have a limited role. Although they can call officials before them to account for actions in their departments, they do not deal with individual grievances of citizens. They act rather as watchdogs, in general over the conduct of administration in a department.

The need was felt for ombudsmen in the public sector because the other checks on preventing the abuse of power and of resolving grievances were seen to be inadequate. However, the ombudsman can operate alongside other methods of dispute resolution and alongside other methods of public law control. Many people believe that the British system of public law is inadequate to contain the powers of a very heavily centralized executive. Rowat (1985: 58) warned against the idea that an ombudsman would cure all administrative ills, arguing that we need a whole variety of controls over administrative action, and other reforms to plug the gaps in our system of control. In fact, the emergence of the Parliamentary Commissioner for Administration in 1967 was accompanied by a debate about the need to reform our system of administrative justice more generally. This was not done, and thus the PCA can be seen as a weak concession to the reformists to avoid a broader re-examination of administrative justice.

Ombudsmen must be seen, therefore, as one among a number of methods of controlling public bodies. They are part of a whole array of controls. The powers granted to the ombudsman allow him or her to address administrative problems that the courts, the legislature and the executive cannot effectively resolve.

THE ROLE OF THE OMBUDSMAN

The modern ombudsman institution is 'primarily a client-oriented office, designed to secure individual justice in the administrative state' (Friedmann 1988: 110). This is certainly true in the UK, where the various public sector ombudsmen were set up as a method of handling individual grievances. However, their work is not confined to individual issues. The individual cases investigated may highlight weaknesses in procedures, practices, rules or attitudes. The ombudsman is concerned that these administrative failures are rectified, so that the same mistakes are not made in the future. Those who have not complained will also be helped by the process of uncovering wrongdoing and poor administration. As well as obtaining redress for the individual complainant, ombudsmen are thus concerned with improving public administration in general, so that future injustice and maladministration will be prevented.

The public sector ombudsmen can thus be seen as having two roles, that of individual grievance redress and that of achieving better administration. These two roles can be complementary, but they can also conflict. For example, ombudsmen, quite rightly, emphasize the importance of the informal settlement of grievances. In these situations, if a settlement is reached that is acceptable to the complainant, the authority and the ombudsman, then 'there is nothing further which needs to be done on the issue in point, and it is unnecessary to draw further attention to the defect which has been discovered' (Yardley 1983: 526). In these cases an individual complainant will be satisfied, but there will not be a thorough investigation of the authority's or department's procedures.

Where the ombudsman identifies injustice to an individual citizen, then clearly the authority concerned should take heed by improving its administration, if only to ensure that the same circumstances do not reoccur. However, as a more general panacea for bad administration the ombudsman has limitations, because there is no roving commission to investigate bad administration. Action can only be taken when a specific individual complaint is made. If more emphasis were placed on improving administration, it might result in a different relationship with public bodies, which might be happy to cooperate with individual grievance redress, but not so happy if the ombudsman had a roving commission to comment upon their procedures.

The British model is basically one of compromise, with some attempt to improve procedures where possible. There are differences of opinion as to how far the ombudsmen should be involved in improving administration. For example, there are some who believe that an efficiency audit is 'a substantial function in its own right to be carried out by an ad hoc body and not to be tied to or seen as a spin-off benefit from investigation into individual complaints' (Moore 1991: 13). On the other hand, it can be argued that one of the primary functions of an ombudsman is to seek out causes of injustice at the systemic level, in the way that a court of law could never do, and that current practice could be greatly improved (Lewis 1992: 4). In fact, in a survey of ombudsmen worldwide, conducted by Haller, 41 of 43 ombudsmen throughout the world said that one of their functions was to improve administrative practices. The same number included proposals for improving legislation and administrative rules as one of their functions. Indeed, only six respondents to the survey regarded the seeking of satisfactory action for the individual as their *prime task*. The majority (27) believed that this task was as important as ensuring that the authorities within their jurisdiction properly fulfilled their duties (Haller 1988: 34–6).

Harlow and Rawlings (1984: 199) discuss the two different roles of ombudsmen, using the model of firefighters and firewatchers. The courts are identified primarily as firefighters, in the sense that judges react to pre-existing disputes. However, in resolving these disputes they establish precedents that may help to prevent future outbreaks. On the other hand, the Council on Tribunals has developed firewatching through persuasion as its key function. Ombudsmen combine elements of both functions, as they exist to resolve grievances (firefighting), but they take a more direct interest than the courts in stimulating administrative improvements (firewatching), and may pursue their goals not only by judgements but also by less formal negotiations or consultations.

Their role as firefighters was largely set by the Whyatt Report (Justice 1961), which recommended that an impartial officer should investigate and report on complaints of maladministration. It took a narrow, grievance redressing view of the function of an ombudsman, and did not even consider the objective of identifying and eradicating administrative inefficiency. Harlow and Rawlings (1984: 207) emphasize the importance of the fire-watching, administration-improving role, believing that the primary role should be that of an independent and unattached investigator, with a mandate to identify maladministration, recommend improved procedures and ensure their implementation. The individual complaint is primarily a mechanism which draws attention to more general administrative deficiencies. However, the problem with using the individual complaint in this way is that unjustified complaints will involve no administrative improvements. It is also a patchy method of drawing attention to administrative defects, as many citizens do not complain (see Harlow 1978: 450–3). Ombudsmen are helped in this aspect of their role if they are entitled to carry out investigations on their own initiative, without the need for an individual complaint. In fact, none of the public sector ombudsmen in the United Kingdom is empowered to conduct 'own initiative' investigations, and in this respect they are out of line with ombudsmen in other systems (Haller 1988: 41–3).

CRITERIA FOR EVALUATION

What criteria should be adopted in order to assess the effectiveness of an ombudsman scheme? One of the great strengths of the ombudsman scheme is the impartial investigation of grievances. Therefore an ombudsman must be independent of the executive and any partisan influence. This independence can be safeguarded in a number of ways. For example, the jurisdiction, powers and method of appointment of an ombudsman should be a matter of public knowledge. Those who appoint the ombudsman should be independent of those who will be subject to investigation, and the appointment must not be subject to premature termination apart from incapacity, misconduct or other good cause. The office should be adequately staffed and financed. Only if the office is seen to be independent will there be increased public confidence in public administration, and a reassurance for the public that official wrongs when discovered will be corrected (see Caiden 1988: 3).

In order to be effective, the ombudsman must have adequate powers of investigation and a jurisdictional coverage which is as wide as possible. Ideally, there should be ombudsmen to cover all types of administrative agencies and all levels of government (Rowat 1985: 183). There should be the right to require the production of all the relevant information and documents to ensure that a thorough examination of the case can be made.

The ombudsman should be able to ensure that there is an effective remedy where administrative shortcomings are found. The public sector ombudsmen do not, in general, make legally binding decisions, but only make recommendations. This is not out of line with ombudsmen worldwide, and it is thought that if there were decision making powers, the institution would become 'entirely and radically different' (Friedmann 1988: 128). If the ombudsman's recommendations are not legally binding, there should be a reasonable expectation that there will be compliance with them, and where there is non-compliance this should be publicized.

Another requirement is accessibility. There is differential use of ombudsmen throughout the world, but in essence 'almost everywhere in the world it is a free public service available at no cost to the complainant' (Moore 1991: 6). One of the great advantages of an ombudsman over other methods of grievance redress is the fact of easy access. Any requirements that a complainant should first exhaust the internal grievance procedures of the body complained against is still in keeping with this requirement. However, it has been argued that complainants must be allowed to go direct to the ombudsman's office rather than being filtered through a Member of Parliament, as they are for complaints to the Parliamentary ombudsman (see Chapter 2). The procedures adopted by ombudsmen must be such that complainants can use them easily, and attention should be paid to particular requirements (for example, that complaints have to be in writing) to ensure that they do not present an obstacle for complainants.

As well as being easily accessible, in order to be effective the ombudsman should be widely known among the general public, and ombudsmen must make every effort to publicize their services. Ombudsmen worldwide are afflicted by the scarcity of public resources, and it is claimed that they 'cannot be as active as they would like in outreach programs' (Caiden 1988: 7). Many ombudsmen seem reluctant to publicize their services for fear of being overloaded, and thus subject to the same kinds of delay and bureaucracy that they are supposed to be curing in the administration. If this is so, remedies must be found, as otherwise the institution, by default, could become another middle-class instrument, which is scarcely used by the disadvantaged and powerless in society. There is a problem of visibility for all the public sector ombudsmen, and serious consideration should be given to raising their profile, by means of outreach work and advertising.

CONCLUSION

In Britain the ombudsman was initially seen as an adjunct to Parliament, whose role was to assist Members of Parliament in their dealings with government agencies on behalf of their constituents (see Rowat 1968). As a method of grievance resolution, the ombudsman is ideally placed to protect the interests of all concerned. The procedure is informal, the wide powers of investigation ensure the ability to uncover the facts, and the office is independent and impartial. These unique characteristics render the office capable of addressing many of the concerns left untouched by the traditional bureaucratic control devices. Citizens can feel confident that maladministration will be uncovered, and officials can feel that, where no maladministration is found, official action is vindicated.

Despite the initial, restricted view of the ombudsman's role, the public sector ombudsmen are becoming involved in improving administration in general. Thus the ombudsman is valuable in obtaining redress for individual citizens, but for citizens at large the value is in encouraging administrative reforms. The ombudsman persuades and recommends, rather than controls, and encourages the use of informal settlements. There is much to be said for the informal settlement of disputes, where this is possible, and where the settlement does not merely cover up systematic maladministration. Negotiated settlements mean that the parties retain control over the outcome of their dispute, but there must be care that the integrity of the office is not compromised, and that settlements are not reached at the expense of a thorough investigation into procedures that are faulty.

Whether the ombudsman should be restricted to cases involving maladministration is a matter of some debate, and will be discussed in the ensuing chapters. Some argue that any extension of this would involve the ombudsman substituting his or her view, and this is politically controversial. Others argue that there should be the power to criticize the use of administrative discretion where it has clearly been unreasonable. It is also thought that the jurisdictional remit is too narrow, and that there should be the power to initiate investigations without the need for an individual complaint.

Ombudsmen should be seen as one form of grievance redress and one method of public law control. There are a number of institutions and organizations for remedying complaints against modern administrative action but, as Rowat (1985: 185) says, 'the ombudsman institution has a unique combination of characteristics that give it advantages over all other types.' Most important is independence, together with the prestige of the office and the powers to investigate and publicize. This gives the institution a strength which non-governmental organizations and even members of a legislature cannot match.

However, there is no room for complacency, and ombudsmen have a number of issues to address. One concerns jurisdiction, and whether the remit should be extended. Should the ombudsman continue to be reactive, or should there be a more proactive role? How formal or informal should the procedures be, and should there be a wide or narrow legalistic view of the ombudsman's powers? There is an issue in relation to resources, in that the ombudsman should have a right of control to ensure adequate staffing levels. Resource matters in general can cause problems for ombudsmen, and can blur the distinction between administration and policy. For example, a complaint may really involve a problem about resource allocation, or a problem may have to be looked at in the context of scarce resources.

There is also an issue of credibility. There is a danger that complainants, and the public at large, may have expectations of ombudsmen which are too high. Any publicity about the institution must guard against raising expectations that are unrealistic. Nevertheless, the public sector ombudsmen do have great potential, and there is scope for development, particularly as a means of improving public administration. These matters will be addressed in the ensuing chapters.

THE PARLIAMENTARY COMMISSIONER FOR ADMINISTRATION

INTRODUCTION

The office of the Parliamentary Commissioner for Administration (PCA) was set up by the Parliamentary Commissioner Act 1967. The Act is largely based on the recommendations made after an inquiry by Justice, whose findings were published in the Whyatt Report, *The Citizen and the Administration*, in 1961. The impetus for such an inquiry was the feeling that there was a gap in the arrangements that existed for redressing grievances or remedying maladministration (Wheare 1973: 112). Justice concluded that the traditional controls on bureaucracy left a gap into which the ombudsman should be inserted. The use of such methods as adjournment debates and Parliamentary questions to control the executive were uneven contests, because only the executive possessed all the relevant information.

This gap had been highlighted by the Franks Committee on Administrative Tribunals and Inquiries, which had reported in 1957. The Franks Committee had been limited by its terms of reference to inquire into disputes in which formal machinery for appeal, or for review before a final decision, already existed, and to suggest improvements in that machinery. The report contained extensive proposals for the improvement of inquiry and tribunal procedures, but could not cover the wider problem of effective machinery for citizen grievances against public authorities, where there was no appeal to an administrative tribunal.

It was acknowledged that some complaints by citizens could be referred to the ordinary courts; some could be dealt with by tribunals set up under statute; some could be referred to a minister after a special procedure had been followed. However, as Franks identified, 'over most of the field of public administration no formal procedure is provided for objecting or deciding on objections' (Franks 1957: para. 10).

The Justice inquiry was therefore set up to

> inquire into the adequacy of the existing means for investigating complaints against administrative acts or decisions of Government Departments and other public bodies, where there is no tribunal or other statutory procedure available for dealing with the complaints; and to consider possible improvements to such means, with particular reference to the Scandinavian institution known as the Ombudsman.
>
> (Justice 1961: terms of reference)

One of the conclusions reached was that there was substantial scope for subjecting a large number of administrative decisions involving discretion to some kind of appeal. In addition, the report addressed the issue of maladministration, that is where there were complaints that an administrative authority had failed to discharge the duties of its office in accordance with proper standards of administrative conduct (Justice 1961: 35). The report concluded that an ombudsman should be appointed to investigate such complaints of maladministration. 'Impartiality and informality' were acknowledged as being 'indispensable characteristics of any machinery' for investigating such complaints (Justice 1961: 36), and the Comptroller and Auditor-General was identified as a model, with the recommendation that the ombudsman should have the same status.

The Comptroller and Auditor-General was established by the Exchequer and Audit Act 1866, with the primary function of auditing the accounts of government departments and certifying them correct or otherwise. She or he is independent of government, and exercises control in financial matters, in effect investigating financial maladministration. Like the Comptroller and Auditor-General, the ombudsman would be answerable to Parliament, but independent of the executive. Initially cases would be investigated at the request of MPs or members of the House of Lords but, as time went on, the public would be able to make complaints direct. It was also recommended that, before commencing an investigation, the Parliamentary Commissioner should notify the minister concerned, who would be entitled to veto the proposed investigation.

The Whyatt proposals were fairly conservative, but were nevertheless rejected by the Conservative government at the time on the grounds that to accept its recommendations would 'seriously interfere with the prompt and efficient despatch of public business' (HC Deb., Vol. 666, Col. 1124).

The succeeding Labour government, however, had committed itself to the proposal in its election manifesto, which promised to 'humanise the whole administration of the state and to set up the new office of Parliamentary Commissioner with the right and duty to investigate and expose any misuse of government power as it affects the citizen' (Labour Party 1964: 3).

Although pledged to introduce this reform, the Labour administration did experience difficulties in introducing the legislation, and the resulting Act is very much a compromise. Indeed, the White Paper (1965) emphasized that the office was intended to enforce the existing constitutional arrangements for protecting individuals. The ombudsman is set very much in a Parliamentary context, with MPs referring cases, and the ombudsman presenting reports to MPs and the House of Commons. Gregory and Hutchesson (1975: 88) have concluded that the ombudsman scheme introduced in Britain was transformed from a public institution readily and directly available to the citizen, to a 'wholly Parliamentary institution, in essence an instrument at the disposal of MPs and designed to help them carry out more effectively their traditional functions on behalf of the citizen.' The office is not a citizen's friend and protector, as it is in Scandinavia and New Zealand (Gregory and Hutchesson 1975: 137).

THE SCHEME

The Act provides for the appointment of the Parliamentary Commissioner, whose function is to investigate administrative action taken on behalf of the Crown. The commissioner is an independent officer of Parliament, and Section 1 of the Act provides that the office is held during good behaviour. A commissioner may be relieved of office by request, but otherwise removal from office before retiring age can only be effected by the Queen on addresses from both Houses of Parliament. This section was amended by Section 2 of the Parliamentary and Health Service Commissioners Act 1987, to enable the removal of a commissioner who is incapable for medical reasons of performing the duties of the office, without the need for addresses from both Houses of Parliament. This would cover the case where a commissioner was so severely incapacitated as to be incapable of resigning, and is included as a precautionary measure. The Parliamentary Commissioner began to investigate complaints on 1 April 1967.

The commissioner is empowered to investigate the government departments and other authorities listed in Schedule 2 of the Parliamentary Commissioner Act 1967. This schedule includes almost all the departments of central government as being subject to investigation. Jurisdiction was extended by Section 2 of the Parliamentary and Health Service Commissioners Act 1987, to cover certain non-departmental bodies, and the complete list is now to be found in Schedule 1 of that Act (Appendix 1 shows the complete list of departments and other authorities subject to investigation).

The authorities within jurisdiction are essentially central government departments and certain non-departmental public bodies. Those added by the 1987 Act were as a result of the undertaking given by the government in the 1985 White Paper, *Non-Departmental Public Bodies*. The criterion for inclusion was that bodies should have executive or administrative functions that directly affect individuals or groups of citizens, and that would be within the Parliamentary Commissioner for Administration's jurisdiction if carried out by a government department. Furthermore, they should be subject to some degree of ultimate ministerial accountability to Parliament, in that they are dependent for their financing and continued existence on government policy (White Paper 1985: para. 3).

Advisory bodies and tribunals were not to be included. This exclusion prevented the Monopolies and Mergers Commission and Boundary Commission being added to the list, as they are deemed to be advisory only. The Criminal Injuries Compensation Board and the Civil Aviation Authority are also excluded, as they are deemed to be tribunals. Some important bodies are, however, included, for example the Urban Development Corporations and the Commission for Racial Equality. Training and Enterprise Councils are not included since they are bodies operating essentially under contract with the minister, but do not operate as his agent. The 'Next Steps' executive agencies are, of course, subject to the jurisdiction of the PCA (*PCA Annual Report* 1990: 2). Indeed, the PCA investigates as many cases involving departmental agencies as he does cases involving the parent departments themselves (*PCA Annual Report* 1991: 2).

Section 1 of the 1987 Act also allows for the Schedule to be amended by Order in Council, to include those bodies where more than half of their running costs come from money provided by Parliament or funds raised under legislative authority. The reference to an authority includes ministers, members or officers of the authority (Section 4, 1967 Act). Section 5 of the 1967 Act extends this by authorizing the PCA to investigate actions taken by or on behalf of an authority. This would therefore include cases where a government department has delegated its functions to another body. Because of the way in which the Parliamentary Commissioner Act 1967 was drafted, new bodies must be specifically brought within the jurisdiction of the PCA before complaints against them can be considered. The present PCA considers this unfortunate, and is hoping that some way can be found of bringing new bodies automatically within jurisdiction, unless, in the legislation establishing them, they are specifically excluded from it (*PCA Annual Report* 1992: 7).

Local authorities are not included, and this exclusion was widely criticized during the passage of the Bill, by members in both Houses, on the grounds that this was an area that produced a number of complaints, many of which were brought to MPs. Local authorities are now subject to the jurisdiction of the Local Government Ombudsman. However, Section 4 of the 1967 Act, as amended by the Parliamentary and Health Service Commissioners Act 1987, provides that the Police Complaints Authority, professional bodies and educational establishments are not within the PCA's jurisdiction. Unlike schools, which are subject to the control of local education authorities, this means that educational establishments for both higher and further education are outside the scope of any ombudsman system.

JURISDICTION

Despite the extensive list of authorities subject to the jurisdiction of the PCA, many areas of government activity are excluded from scrutiny, and it has been said that from the outset the limitations on jurisdiction have been one of the most widely criticized features of the scheme (Gregory and Hutchesson 1975: 178). Section 5(3) of the 1967 Act provides that the commissioner shall not investigate any action or matter described in Schedule 3. Schedule 3 contains eleven 'Matters not subject to investigation', and this has the effect of eliminating large areas, in many departments, from investigation. These will be examined in turn.

Foreign affairs (para. 1). Although the Foreign Office is included in Schedule 2 as a department subject to investigation, this paragraph empowers the Foreign Secretary or other ministers to prevent an investigation into a matter which affects relations or dealings between the government and overseas governments or international organizations.

Actions overseas (para. 2). Action taken outside the United Kingdom (UK) by British officials was in general excluded, so that complaints about the actions of staff at British embassies, missions and consulates abroad could not be investigated. The Channel Islands and the Isle of Man are regarded as territories outside the UK, for the purpose of this exclusion. However, cases involving the actions of career consular officials overseas in relation to UK citizens were brought within the PCA's jurisdiction by Statutory Instrument No. 915 of 1979. The Parliamentary Commissioner (Consular Complaints) Act 1981 further extended the PCA's jurisdiction, so as to enable British citizens resident overseas to make complaints about the quality of the assistance they receive from consular officials.

Colonial government (para. 3). This paragraph prevents any investigation of action taken in connection with the administration of the government of any country or territory outside the UK, where the UK has jurisdiction, for example colonies or protectorates. Actions taken in the UK in connection with these matters is covered by the exclusion, as well as actions taken abroad.

Extradition (para. 4). This refers to actions taken by the Home Secretary under the Extradition Act 1870 and the Fugitive Offenders Act 1881, in relation to confirming or rejecting orders of extradition.

Investigating crime (para. 5). Although the Home Office is included, this paragraph prevents the investigation of the actions of the Home Secretary for the purpose of investigating crime or of protecting the security of the state. It should be noted that the PCA has no power to investigate the actions of the police, and this exclusion therefore relates to certain specific actions by the Home Secretary, for example the authorization of telephone tapping. The paragraph also specifically mentions the power to withdraw or withhold passports in connection with these matters. The exercise of the power to issue or deny passports is, however, judicially reviewable (see *R* v. *Secretary of State for Foreign and Commonwealth Affairs: ex parte Everett* (1987), *The Independent* 4 December 1987).

Criminal or civil court proceedings (para. 6). This paragraph prevents the commissioner investigating the commencement or conduct of civil or criminal proceedings before the courts in the UK, proceedings in military courts and proceedings before any international court or tribunal. This exclusion covers the decision by departments on whether or not to commence proceedings.

It should be added that there had been a dispute for a number of years between the PCA and the Lord Chancellor's Department concerning jurisdiction over complaints about the administrative actions of courts staff. Although the Lord Chancellor's Department is listed in Schedule 2, the department maintained that the courts are separate and independent institutions, and therefore not within the PCA's jurisdiction. This problem has been solved by Section 110 of the Courts and Legal Services Act 1990, which provides that administrative functions exercisable by a person appointed by the Lord Chancellor as a member of the administrative staff of any court or tribunal shall, in the normal course of events, be subject to the investigation of the PCA. Action which is not within jurisdiction is that taken on the authority of a judge.

The change came into effect on 1 January 1991, but there are still inconsistencies. Court staff in Scotland are not included, as there is a different method of organizing courts in Scotland and staff there are under judicial control. Tribunals whose staff are not appointed by the Lord Chancellor are not within the jurisdiction. This is not because it is thought they should not be investigated, but because what is needed is some legislative enactment to remedy this omission (see *PCA Annual Report* 1991: 24). Section 110 goes some way to ending the long-running dispute over the ability to investigate the actions of court staff, and was welcomed by the Select Committee on the Parliamentary Commissioner. The Select Committee has recommended that the anomaly in relation to the staff of tribunals be remedied as soon as possible, if necessary, by primary legislation (HC 158, 1992: para. 12).

Prerogative of mercy (para. 7). Although the Home Office is included, the PCA is prevented from investigating the exercise of the prerogative of mercy by the Home Secretary, which is a discretionary power and cannot be challenged even in Parliament. Also excluded is investigation into the review of a decision on whether to refer a case to the Court of Appeal, the High Court or the Court-Martial Appeal Court.

The National Health Service (para. 8). Although the Ministry of Health (now the Department of Health) is included in the list of departments to be investigated, this paragraph excludes from jurisdiction actions taken by any hospital authority in the National Health Service. This exclusion was defended at the time of the passing of the Act on the basis that hospitals are independent, and more local, and that they had improved procedures for dealing with complaints. However, there were criticisms of this exclusion, and it has been remedied by the introduction of the Health Service Commissioner in 1973. The National Health Service Reorganisation Act 1973 and the National Health Service, Scotland, Act 1973 established the office of the commissioner to examine complaints against hospital authorities. This will be discussed in the next chapter.

Commercial matters (para. 9). All contractual or commercial transactions by government departments or authorities are excluded, except for transactions in the compulsory purchase or disposal of land. This appears to be a wide exclusion, but has accounted for few rejections, perhaps because its scope has been limited by successive PCAs, who have decided that a service does not become 'commercial' because a charge is made for it. This means that such services as the provision of driving tests and licences, the provision of passports and the protection of patents, all of which entail the payment of a fee, are not covered by this exclusion.

It also seems that the exclusion will not apply to cases where the issue is about the landlord and tenant relationship, or licences in connection with land. Acquisition and disposal of land compulsorily is not excluded from investigation, and there have been investigations about the procedure for compulsory purchase and about refusals to purchase in advance of a compulsory purchase programme, and action in connection with blight notices. The justification given for the exclusion is that the PCA's remit should be limited to complaints against government by an aggrieved citizen, rather than by an aggrieved supplier of goods and services.

This exclusion has been criticized, notably by Justice (1977), the Royal Commission on Standards of Conduct in Public Life (Royal Commission 1976) and one of the ombudsmen, Cecil Clothier, in his final report on the PCA (HC 322, 1984). The Select Committee on the Parliamentary Commissioner has recommended that the PCA should be able to investigate complaints where a department has been improperly influenced in deciding which firms to include among those entitled to tender for contracts, or where decisions had been made in an arbitrary manner, or where a department had acted improperly in connection with the withdrawal of a firm's name from the list of approved tenderers.

The government has argued that commercial relations and grants to industry, using statutory powers that involve a wide measure of commercial discretion, should not be subject to review by the PCA (Government Observations 1979). Clearly there are some contractual matters that are more appropriately dealt with by litigation, but this is not a valid reason for excluding the whole administrative side of contracting from the remit of the PCA. The exclusion does involve some strained interpretations as to what is within and without jurisdiction. For example, complaints about the communication of confidential information by one department to another could be investigated, as administrative actions, but if the information is used to remove a contractor from the list of tenderers it becomes a commercial matter, and therefore outside jurisdiction.

The government is, however, unwilling to have its commercial and contractual relationships subjected to scrutiny by the PCA, because it does not consider that these affairs are of the very nature of government. However, it could be argued that it is the exercise of the power of government that is in question here, albeit a power that is exercised through the medium of contract, and that this power is inadequately supervised (see Birkinshaw 1985: 133). Despite the criticisms of the exclusion, there has been little progress in this area, and the present PCA admits that it is 'something of a grey area' (HC 353, 1990: para. 5).

Personnel matters (para. 10). Another controversial exclusion is that provided by paragraph 10, which excludes the investigation of complaints in personnel matters made by civil servants, by other people 'in office or employment' under the Crown and by members of the armed forces. This exclusion has been criticized, but the government's view is that the ombudsman scheme is concerned with the relationship between government and the governed, and not between the state as employer and its employees. To have such jurisdiction would make civil servants a privileged class of employee and, moreover, the existing internal arrangements to deal with staff difficulties through the Whitley Council machinery are more appropriate.

This argument ignores the fact that MPs can, and do, take up cases from civil servants in connection with their employment, and ombudsmen in other countries have such power. The Select Committee has concluded that this exclusion is not justified, particularly in relation to matters prior to appointment to the civil service, and after retirement (HC 129, 1991: para. 9). The exclusion means that action taken in respect of appointments, removals, pay, discipline, superannuation, promotion or postings is excluded. Also excluded are complaints of ex-employees, and even complaints arising after the death of an ex-employee. This exclusion has also been interpreted to cover prospective employees, although this is not necessary on a strict construction of the Act.

Grants of honours (para. 11). The PCA is prevented from investigating the granting of honours, awards or privileges within the gift of the Crown, including the grant of Royal Charters. These particular exercises of prerogative are also probably excluded from judicial review.

These Schedule 3 exclusions were criticized during the passage of the Bill. Some have been remedied, particularly in relation to the exclusion of local authorities and the health service. The exclusion of complaints against the police was partially remedied by the Police Act 1976, which provided for three-person tribunals (two laypersons and the chief constable of the police force concerned) to hear complaints against the police where the case had not been referred to the Director of Public Prosecutions. The Police and Criminal Evidence Act 1984 introduced a revised complaints procedure, with a three-tier system of complaints handling. The Police Complaints Board is now renamed the Police Complaints Authority, and the authority consists of a chairperson and eight other members.

It is noteworthy that in Sweden and Denmark there is a presumption in favour of decisions of public servants being subject to investigation by the ombudsman, unless there is sound reason to the contrary. The Select Committee believes that a similar presumption should and could operate in this country, so that all decisions of civil servants and others within appropriate departments, involving maladministration, should be subject to investigation unless there is a constitutional principle that dictates otherwise (HC 129, 1991: para 9). As the PCA was to strengthen the machinery of Parliamentary surveillance over administrative action by providing MPs with a new instrument for investigating executive action, there can be no case in principle for excluding from the PCA's remit anything that MPs could take up with ministers (see Gregory and Pearson 1992: 489). To adopt the Swedish and Danish principle would widen the PCA's jurisdiction, increase the numbers of cases referred to, and investigated by, the office and do much to remove the restricted nature of the PCA's remit. The restrictions imposed reduce the value of the office, and their removal would seem to be a way forward.

There is no equivalent restriction on the PCA to that on the Local Government Ombudsman to prevent an investigation of matters that concern all or most of the inhabitants of an area. However, what are excluded are matters that are purely 'political', which is interpreted as matters that have been debated in Parliament. Indeed cases of complaints where MPs have tried and failed in an adjournment debate to secure redress cannot be investigated, even where there is *prima facie* evidence of maladministration and injustice (Rawlings 1986a: 141).

DISCRETIONARY POWERS

Under the 1967 Act, the ombudsman cannot investigate any administrative action in respect of which the person aggrieved has or had a right to go before a tribunal or had a remedy in a court of law (Section 5(2)). The proviso to this section is that the ombudsman can do so where he or she is satisfied that, in the particular circumstances, the individual cannot reasonably be expected to resort to this remedy. In practice the PCA often refuses to investigate where there is a right of appeal to a tribunal. However, where the remedy is in court, unless it is a case which is well within the jurisdiction of the court, for example personal injuries, the PCA will usually investigate (see Justice 1988: 95). One of the previous ombudsmen has said that if there were any doubt about the availability of a legal remedy, or the process of law seemed too cumbersome, slow and expensive for the objective to be gained, he would exercise his discretion in favour of the complainant (HC 148, 1981: 1).

Even if a complaint is within jurisdiction, the PCA still has discretion whether or not to investigate. Section 5(1) of the 1967 Act says that the commissioner *may* investigate, and this is emphasized by Section 5(5), which says that the commissioner shall act 'in accordance with his own discretion' and that the commissioner is to decide whether a complaint is duly made.

The courts will not interfere with this discretion. In *Re Fletcher* [1970] 2 All ER 527, the applicant wanted a court order requiring the ombudsman to hear his allegations of neglect of duty. The House of Lords concluded that they had no jurisdiction to order the PCA to investigate any complaint, saying that they were bound by the Act, and that as they took the view that the ombudsman has a discretion whether to investigate a complaint or not, there was nothing they could do about it. They therefore refused to require the PCA to investigate the complaint.

This view was confirmed in the recent case of *R* v. *PCA ex parte Lithgow and another* (1990, unreported), where the Queen's Bench Division refused to interfere with the decision of the PCA not to investigate a complaint. Indeed, doubt was expressed by the court as to whether they would interfere with the PCA's decision on his own jurisdiction in any event, and a distinction was drawn between the PCA and the Local Government Ombudsman in this respect. Decisions by the Local Government Ombudsman have been considered by the court where there has been a dispute over jurisdiction (see Chapter 4), but in the *Lithgow* case it was thought that questions relating to jurisdiction should not be investigated by the court unless the matter fell within the principles of *Wednesbury* unreasonableness. Presumably, where a department thought that the PCA had no jurisdiction to investigate, a declaratory judgement as to the scope of jurisdiction would be sought. However, as there has been no such case so far in relation to the PCA, the outcome of such a course of action is uncertain.

Section 6(3) of the Act requires that the complaint be received by the MP within twelve months of the time the complainant became aware, or ought to have become aware, of the matters about which she or he is complaining. This does not bar investigations of actions that took place before the previous twelve months, as time only begins to run when the alleged injustice comes to light. The PCA has a discretion to investigate complaints out of time where there are 'special circumstances which make it proper to do so'. This will only be done in certain limited circumstances, for example where the complainant was prevented from making the complaint through illness. Another situation is where a complainant has pursued other remedies unsuccessfully. Once the complaint has been received by the MP, the MP can bring it to the PCA for investigation at any time.

MALADMINISTRATION

The 1967 Act clearly states in Section 5(1) that the ombudsman may investigate a written complaint 'made to a member of the House of Commons by a member of the public who claims to have sustained injustice in consequence of maladministration' by a government department or any other authority named in the Act.

The Whyatt Report had recommended that the ombudsman's jurisdiction should be limited to cases involving maladministration, although it was admitted that the term was 'not one of precise meaning' and that, from the communications received during the course of their inquiry, there was 'considerable confusion as to what matters fall within its scope' (Justice 1961: 34). It should also be noted that, in addition, Whyatt had suggested an extension of the administrative tribunal system, which would have meant that more administrative decisions would have become reviewable. In the UK there is no system for a general appeal on the merits of decisions. If there were such a system, confining the ombudsman to cases of maladministration would not be so restrictive.

Maladministration is the key concept in the Act, which makes its meaning crucially important. Whyatt concluded that it should cover situations where 'an administrative authority has failed to discharge the duties of its office in accordance with proper standards of administrative conduct' (Justice 1961: 35). However, in order to make sure that maladministration was not given too wide an interpretation, an amendment was introduced at the Report Stage of the Bill, which stated that nothing in Section 5 should be construed as authorizing or requiring the commissioner to review by way of appeal any decision taken by a government department or other authority in the exercise of a discretion vested in that department or authority.

This limitation was criticized for being too wide, and was therefore deleted. What was inserted was a clause excluding the ombudsman from reviewing a discretionary decision taken without maladministration. Thus Section 12(3) of the Act states that 'nothing in this Act authorises or requires the Commissioner to question the merits of a decision taken without maladministration by a government department or other authority in the exercise of a discretion vested in that department or authority', which is less restrictive.

Despite the use of the term 'maladministration', and in common with other legislation concerning the public sector ombudsmen, maladministration is not defined in the Act. The omission is deliberate, and it has been left to each ombudsman to decide on the scope of the term. In answer to a question by a member of the Select Committee on the Parliamentary Commissioner for Administration in 1968, Sir Edmund Compton, the first Parliamentary Commissioner, admitted: 'Nobody can define maladministration in plain terms' (HC 350, 1968: Minutes of Evidence, Qu. 151). What is clear is the area of activity that is excluded from the ombudsman's remit. First, the PCA cannot investigate a complaint about the terms of a statute, and no authority can be criticized for acting within its provisions. Similarly, disputes about statutory interpretation are outside the ombudsman's remit.

The ombudsman is not entitled to investigate matters that call into question the policies of a particular authority. Once it is ascertained what a particular policy is, all that the ombudsman can do is check that it has been properly applied in the individual case. However, what the PCA can criticize is where a policy is not properly expressed, or where policies are inconsistent. She or he can also criticize the so-called 'bad rule'. This means that the PCA can examine the effects of a departmental rule allegedly causing hardship to a complainant. If the rule were found by the department to be defective, the PCA could ask what action had been taken to remedy the hardship. If the rule had not been revised, it would be open to the PCA to find maladministration in the individual case if there had been deficiencies in the departmental review of the rule (see Birkinshaw 1985: 135).

Section 12(3), mentioned above, makes it clear that discretionary decisions are not reviewable in the absence of administrative failure. The PCA cannot be used as an appeal from administrative decisions, although he or she can check that the decision was reached in the correct manner, following the correct procedures. In the absence of any error, the ombudsman cannot substitute his or her own opinion, even where she or he clearly disagrees with the decision. Even in cases where there has been maladministration in the manner of reaching the decision, all that the PCA can do is to request that a fresh decision is made in a properly administered manner. He or she cannot overturn that decision.

What kinds of activities will, therefore, come within the ambit of maladministration? Its scope is indicated in the famous 'Crossman catalogue', set out by the late Richard Crossman when he presented the Second Reading of the Parliamentary Commissioner Bill in the House of Commons:

> We might have made an attempt in this clause to define, by catalogue, all of the qualities which make up maladministration, which might count for maladministration by a civil servant. It would be a wonderful exercise – bias, neglect, inattention, delay, incompetence, ineptitude, perversity, turpitude, arbitrariness, and so on.

In practice, it often includes some fairly minor matters, for example losing a file or a letter, mistakes in calculations, or some other human error that leads to the complaint of maladministration. It can cover administrative action or inaction, based on or influenced by improper considerations or conduct. Such improper considerations would include arbitrariness, malice, bias or unfair discrimination. Neglect, unjustifiable delay, incompetence, failure to observe relevant rules and procedures, and failure to take relevant considerations into account are all examples of improper conduct. Officials must act in compliance with the law and departmental rules, and a failure to establish a review procedure where there is a duty to do so or the use of faulty systems are examples of maladministration. In addition, high standards of integrity, efficiency and honesty are expected from officials.

However, these are just examples of maladministration, and the definition used by each ombudsman is crucial to his or her work. The ombudsman has to decide when a delay becomes unjustifiable and therefore maladministration, for example, or whether a particular error is excusable. In some cases there can be an objective assessment, so that actions clearly contrary to the law would be maladministration, as would actions that failed to comply with the rules or procedures of the department.

Given that it is for each ombudsman to decide what conduct is acceptable, within the rules laid down by statute and the Select Committee, the concept of maladministration is not fixed, but is developing. The view of the ombudsmen is therefore crucial. Sir Edmund Compton, the first Parliamentary Commissioner, interpreted maladministration in procedural terms only, maintaining that he should not review discretionary decisions taken without maladministration. The Treasury distinguishes ten types of maladministration (see Stacey 1978: 157), nine of which are procedural, including delays, failure to reply to letters and giving misleading advice. The tenth is bias on the part of an official.

The Select Committee on the Parliamentary Commissioner has not taken so restricted a view, and has said that there are some situations where decisions can be criticized. The Committee has advised the PCA that 'if he finds a decision which, judged by its effect on the aggrieved person, appears to be thoroughly bad in quality, he may infer from the quality of the decision itself' that there had been an element of maladministration in the taking of it and ask for its review (HC 350, 1968: para. 14). In effect, it is saying that even a decision which is procedurally correct could be said to be maladministration if it was thoroughly bad in its effects. However, to come within this provision a decision would have to be so bad that it indicated bias, or even perversity or corruption.

Cecil Clothier's view of maladministration was influenced by resource restraints and recruitment difficulties. He decided that 'unreasonable delay' in itself was not sufficient to constitute maladministration. It would only be so where it was not caused by uncontrollable difficulties in recruitment, 'financial constraints' or 'resource problems beyond the control of the department'. He did not feel justified in criticizing a department which was doing its best in difficult circumstances (HC 258, 1982: 14; HC 419, 1982: 15).

The limitation on investigations to cases involving maladministration has not been without criticism. Justice (1977) has proposed that the ombudsman should not be so limited, and that the term 'maladministration' should be replaced by 'unreasonable, unjust or oppressive action'. (see Harlow and Rawlings 1984: 209). Such a power would be more like that of the New Zealand ombudsman, who can report on decisions which are 'unreasonable, unjust, oppressive or improperly discriminatory', or even 'wrong'. However, the Select Committee in its detailed *Review of Access and Jurisdiction* (HC 615, 1978) saw no need to change this aspect of the PCA's jurisdiction, but accepted that the interpretation of maladministration used by the PCA approximated to the proposed reformulation by Justice. In its most recent review of administrative law, Justice (1988) accepted that no change was needed to the wording of the statute in relation to 'maladministration'. Cecil Clothier, the ombudsman at the time of the review, found the statutory test a 'wholly adequate basis for his investigations' (Justice 1988: 93), and the conclusion reached was that it was sufficiently flexible and wide-ranging in operation, and that its meaning was sufficiently well understood (Justice 1988: 138). A previous ombudsman was of the same opinion, maintaining that he was clear that he 'could now certainly investigate any unjust or oppressive action' (Pugh 1978: 132).

In the ombudsman's reports themselves, the term maladministration is not always used. What are mentioned are 'failings' found on the part of government departments, 'failures' to warn the public, 'failure' to commission tests. It does not necessarily say that this constitutes maladministration, and it therefore seems that the ombudsman is not required to say in the report whether or not he finds maladministration. There may be advantages in finding failings, but not saying whether or not there has been maladministration, and indeed the Act does not require the ombudsman to do so. However, much does depend on the view of the PCA, and the concept of maladministration contained in the legislation could be interpreted narrowly. Staff in the PCA's office may not be trained to think about improving administration and the administrative quality of the decision, but they may place more emphasis on the technical correctness of a decision.

INJUSTICE

An aggrieved person must claim to have sustained 'injustice in consequence of maladministration' (Section 5(1)), and this concept of injustice is central to the work of the PCA. Like maladministration, injustice is not defined in the 1967 Act, and very little was said in Parliament during the passage of the Bill about injustice. It is wider in scope than 'loss' or 'damage', and it was intended that it should be wide enough to cover situations where a person had not suffered financially, even to the extent of a sense of indignation or outrage. In practice, it has been given a wide interpretation, and injustice has been found where the effect was annoyance, as well as the more straightforward cases of financial loss or missed opportunity. However, injustice is not found merely because there is a finding that there has been maladministration. There has to be something over and above this. It has been said that the complainant must show some injustice 'which is personal to him and distinguishes him from the generality of the community' (Clothier 1984: 3109).

There can thus be findings of maladministration but no injustice, as where, for example, there have been some procedural shortcomings in the way a decision was reached, but the result would still have been the same without these shortcomings. In other words, the errors had not affected the correctness of the decision. A person might also receive more favourable treatment owing to some administrative error. Again, there is no question of injustice.

However, there are cases where administrative shortcomings have been said to give rise to injustice, even though the final decision may not have been affected. For example, it has been held to be injustice where an individual, through maladministration, has been denied the opportunity to object to development by a third party. This is seen as a loss of a right, and therefore injustice. Indeed, it has been argued that 'if justice requires that "every man be given his due", and if everyone who deals with government departments is entitled to have his case decided in the proper manner, then defective procedure always constitutes at the same time both maladministration and injustice' (Gregory and Hutchesson 1975: 331). There have been cases where the PCA has taken this view. However, there are also situations where inconvenience and annoyance have not been seen to be sufficient to find injustice.

Injustice has been found in cases of delay or refusal of benefits and refusal or delay in returning erroneous payments. Where financial loss is caused by delay, misleading advice or other wrongful action, this will be injustice. Casting unjustified doubts on a person's honesty or integrity has been held to be injustice, as has unfair prejudicial treatment in connection with appeals.

REMEDIES

It is only when there has been injustice found as a consequence of maladministration that a complainant is entitled to a remedy. In the majority of cases accepted for investigation, the complaint is found to be either wholly or partly justified, as Table 1 indicates. However, the ombudsman has no power to order compensation or other action to remedy the injustice. Any payments made by a department are *ex gratia*. There is no power for the ombudsman to institute proceedings in court or in a tribunal on behalf of the complainant. All that the ombudsman can do is request or recommend

Table 1   Investigation results

Result of investigation	1992	1991	1990	1989	1988
Complaint wholly justified	54	47	42	48	49
Complaint partly justified	39	43	47	42	40
Complaint not justified	7	10	11	10	11

Values are percentages.
Source: PCA Annual Reports

the action the department should take, and it is for the department itself to respond as it thinks fit.

Although it is for the department to provide a remedy, the ombudsman sometimes takes the initiative, and indicates what would be considered a suitable remedy, for example an apology, an apology plus an *ex gratia* payment or a review of procedures. Compensation will only be recommended where it is the appropriate remedy for the injustice caused, for example where a complainant has suffered financial loss through relying on incorrect advice from an official, or where money has been improperly withheld.

Ex gratia payments are not automatically given simply because there has been a finding of injustice as a consequence of maladministration. Other remedies, like a new decision or a review, may be more appropriate. In some cases, an investigation may show that a rule produces consequences which were not intended, and which give rise to hardship or unfairness. Justice (1988) considered whether the ombudsman should be expressly authorized by statute to draw Parliament's attention to such cases, which expose a defect in the law. However, the PCA does already point out these cases of unfairness that result from legislation, and can notify the Law Commission of cases where the investigation has suggested that the law is defective or unjust. There is therefore no need for the 1967 Act to be amended (Justice 1988: 92).

There are cases where the department does not accept the PCA's conclusions and recommendations. This happened in the Sachsenhausen case and the Court Line case, and, more recently, in the case of Barlow Clowes. The Sachsenhausen case involved the refusal of the Foreign Office to pay compensation to a number of former servicemen, who claimed to have been victims of Nazi persecution by virtue of their detention in Sachsenhausen concentration camp during the Second World War. The complainants' case was taken up by MPs, but to no avail, and in June 1967 the case was submitted to the PCA for investigation. The commissioner reported in December 1967, and found that there had been injustice as a consequence of maladministration by the department, on the grounds that the department had taken into account irrelevant information when reaching its decision, and had failed to take into account all the relevant information. The Foreign Secretary dismissed the findings of maladministration and disagreed with the ombudsman's conclusions and criticisms. However, despite this, he reversed the decisions of the department and awarded compensation to the complainants.

The Court Line case concerned the collapse of the Court Line travel business in 1974. A number of MPs received complaints from individuals, who felt that the Department of Industry was partly to blame for their losses sustained at the collapse. The PCA investigated, and his investigation became the subject of a special report (*Fifth Report* 1974–5), in which it was concluded that the government could not be absolved from all responsibility for the losses. He criticized ministerial statements made some two months before the collapse, saying that they were likely to have left the public with a misleading impression. It was felt that the government gave a misleading guarantee of the soundness of Court Line, and thereby misled people into investing money in a company that failed. The government rejected the PCA's findings, considering it a matter of political judgement, and departmental action was defended in Parliament. The government, therefore, did not feel that it was appropriate to accept any financial responsibility for the losses caused by the collapse, and no remedy was forthcoming for the complainants (HC 498, 1975).

In the Barlow Clowes case the government rejected the PCA's findings but nevertheless paid the complainants compensation, in what was described by the PCA as 'the most substantial financial remedy ever to result from an investigation' (HC 353, 1990: paras 7, 64). This case involved complaints from investors in the Barlow Clowes Investment Group, following its collapse. The case arose because, under the Prevention of Fraud (Investments) Act 1958, it was an offence for anyone to carry on the business of dealing in securities without a licence. Licences were issued by the Secretary of State for Trade and Industry, whose department also had some monitoring functions over those to whom it issued a licence.

The complainants' case was that they had incurred financial loss, owing to maladministration in the way that the Department of Trade and Industry had regulated the Barlow Clowes Investment Group. The PCA reported in 1989, and identified five areas where there had been significant maladministration by the Department that had contributed substantially to the investors' losses. In particular, the Department could have monitored more closely the activities of the group, and could have withdrawn the licence.

The government disagreed with the Commissioner's findings, arguing that the Department's actions had been of a reasonably acceptable standard, and that no financial regulator could, or should, guarantee the safety of investors' funds. The government also believed that the PCA should not be investigating cases where the complainants had no direct relationship with the relevant government department. Despite this, the government agreed to make substantial *ex gratia* payments to all investors who had suffered loss as a result of the collapse of Barlow Clowes.

If a department refuses to follow the recommendation of the ombudsman, there is nothing a complainant can do to obtain redress. In individual cases, the Select Committee on the Parliamentary Commissioner can comment on the matter, and individual MPs can take up the matter in the House of Commons in an adjournment debate, for example. But there is no formal sanction attached to the recommendations, and solutions need to be negotiated where they are not readily forthcoming.

Justice (1988: 103) examined the remedies available to the ombudsman, and discussed whether the recommendations of the PCA should be enforceable through the courts. The argument for such a power is that the injustice remains unremedied if the department refuses to comply with the recommendations. But the enforceability of remedies has not been a problem for the PCA, and departments do tend to comply. This is largely due to the existence of the Select Committee, backed up by the authority of Parliament. Political factors also play a part. This is particularly illustrated in cases like Barlow Clowes, where the government rejected the PCA's findings, but nevertheless made *ex gratia* payments.

One of the strengths of the present system is that departments remain fully responsible, and the PCA relies on their cooperation, both in carrying out investigations and at the remedy stage. To have judicial enforcement may lead to departments demanding a right of appeal, and it would certainly alter the essential aspect of the office, which is cooperation. This cooperation is seen to be the key to the ombudsman's success, which enforcement through the courts may jeopardize (Justice 1988: 104).

PROCEDURE AND POWERS

Section 5(1) of the 1967 Act allows the ombudsman to investigate written complaints made by a member of the public to a Member of Parliament, provided the complaint is referred by the MP, who requests the investigation, and the person who made it consents to the investigation. Access is therefore only through MPs, an issue which will be taken up later in the chapter. When a complaint is received in the PCA's office from an MP, it is first screened to see if it is within jurisdiction.

Appendix II of the PCA's First Report (*PCA Annual Report* 1967–8) lists the tests that will be used in the screening process. The first is given above: according to the Act a complaint will only be within the jurisdiction of the PCA if an MP requests an investigation, and the complainant consents to the investigation. The mandatory provisions of the Act require that it has to concern administrative actions by or on behalf of the departments or authorities listed in Schedule 2 of the Act, but that the action is not excluded by Schedule 3. The complainant must not be excluded by Section 6(1); that is, the complainant cannot be a local authority or other public body. The complaint must be by, or on behalf of, an aggrieved person who is resident or present in the UK, or the complaint must relate to an action taken while she or he was present in this country (Section 6(2)). This provision covers situations of temporary visits, and also covers those who are in this country illegally. Indeed, a number of complaints about the action of immigration officers rest on this assumption, and they have been investigated. In addition, the complaint must be brought to an MP within the twelve months time limit and there must be no remedy to be found in the courts or tribunals, although the PCA has discretion to investigate in these two situations.

The PCA in office at the time of writing, William Reid, emphasizes the key role played by the screening unit in his office, the function of which is not to investigate, but to appraise new complaints. On the basis of this appraisal, the PCA decides whether to investigate (*PCA Annual Report* 1991: 29). The PCA may decline to investigate in the case of repeat complaints unless new evidence has arisen. Those considered frivolous or vexatious would not be investigated, although in practice few of these would pass the MP filter. The PCA may refuse to investigate where the complaint is essentially about political judgement, and it would therefore be inappropriate to comment. If nothing is to be gained by the investigation, then the PCA will use his discretion to decline to investigate. Sometimes investigations are discontinued at the request of the MP or complainant, where, for example, a settlement is reached with the department. In 1991, the target time for the screening process was three and a half weeks (*PCA Annual Report* 1991: 50), and the target time for the next three years is three weeks (*PCA Annual Report* 1992: 57).

Where the ombudsman declines to investigate, he or she is required to send a statement of reasons to the MP referring the case. There is no obligation to send this to the body complained against. In contrast, where the Health Service Commissioner rejects complaints, the statement of reasons for not investigating the complaint has to be sent to the complainant and body complained against. In practice, only about one in four of complaints referred by MPs will get to the stage of a full investigation (*PCA Annual Report* 1991: 30).

When the complaint is accepted for investigation, this fact is reported to the referring MP, and the investigatory process begins. The first stage of this process involves the ombudsman referring the complaint to the principal officer of the relevant department for comments. This is a requirement of the Act, Section 7(1) providing that the principal officer of the department complained against has to have an opportunity to comment upon any allegation contained in a complaint accepted for investigation. Other officers named in the complaint are also invited by the principal officer to contact the ombudsman, if the ombudsman wishes, to give comments. Replies are usually requested within a fortnight, but in practice, they may take longer, although there is an expectation that the ombudsman will receive initial comments from departments within an absolute maximum of six weeks. Departments usually comply with this timescale (*PCA Annual Report* 1991: 5). The replies provide a thorough account of the case, and with this information the PCA's staff decide whether it should be pursued, or whether for jurisdictional or other reasons (for example, if a satisfactory remedy is offered) it ought to be discontinued.

Most cases accepted for investigation proceed beyond stage 1 and, if it is decided to continue with the investigation, the second stage of the process begins. The procedure for investigation is for the PCA to determine, but Section 7(2) of the Act requires that the investigation be held in private. Only very rarely will the PCA come to a conclusion on the basis of the principal officers' replies alone. In the normal course of events, the PCA's staff examine the departmental files and interview the officers involved in the case. Occasionally it may be necessary to interview ministers.

The case papers can be sent to the ombudsman's office, or ombudsman's staff will visit the department. William Reid is concerned that departments and other authorities are taking steps to keep case papers for a shorter time than formerly, in order to reduce the volume of records they retain. This may affect the ability to investigate complaints thoroughly, as may the trend towards electronic communications and record keeping. He suggests that if departmental documents crucial to the resolution of a complaint have been destroyed, he may in some circumstances give the complainant the benefit of the doubt, if there is no documentary evidence to refute the complainant's story (*PCA Annual Report* 1991: 5–6).

Complainants will also be interviewed by the PCA's staff, usually in their own homes, and sometimes in the presence of their MP or another adviser. The PCA has a discretion to allow representation by a lawyer or otherwise, and this applies not only to the complainant but also to officers involved in the investigation. Section 7(3) gives power to the ombudsman to pay towards any expenses incurred in connection with an investigation. These include travelling expenses and any loss of earnings to attend for interview. In practice there will be little cause for expenditure, as people are usually interviewed in their own homes or places of work. Where a professional representative is used, the ombudsman has the power to pay towards the reasonable cost of such representation.

Section 8 of the 1967 Act gives the PCA extensive powers to ensure that she or he can conduct a full investigation. Any person, including a minister, can be required to give information or produce documents that are relevant to the investigation. Witnesses can be compelled to attend and give evidence, in the same way that the High Court can compel, and the ombudsman has the power to administer oaths. There is no obligation on civil servants to maintain secrecy and no restriction upon the disclosure of information applies to information disclosed to the ombudsman. Nor can Crown privilege be used to withhold documents or evidence.

These powers are very wide, and they are backed by the power, contained in Section 9, to certify that obstructions, acts or omissions would constitute a contempt of court, if the proceedings were taking place in court. The court can then deal with the matter, after a hearing, as if it were a contempt of court. The powers are, however, subject to exceptions. First, Section 8(5) ensures that a person cannot be compelled to give evidence or produce documents that he or she could not be compelled to do in proceedings before the High Court. Second, Section 8(4) provides that information relating to proceedings of the Cabinet, or any Cabinet committee, cannot be produced. In these cases the Secretary of the Cabinet, with the approval of the Prime Minister, can certify that information relates to the Cabinet, and this is conclusive. This restriction has apparently not caused any problems in practice.

Although the Act gives the ombudsman a power to see all the documents in the case, Section 11(3) empowers a minister to instruct the commissioner not to disclose the contents of a document on the grounds that disclosure would be 'prejudicial to the safety of the State or otherwise contrary to the public interest'. This power has rarely been used, and in other respects the PCA is stronger than many other ombudsmen in other systems. For example, she or he can criticize the actions of ministers on the same grounds as those of civil servants.

This system of investigation, involving as it does the sending of investigators to departments to examine files, and if necessary to interview officials, is very time consuming. The investigations are very much of a 'Rolls-Royce' standard, involving a high-level review, with each investigation coming to the attention of the permanent secretary in the department. Most other ombudsmen systems employ a less vigorous method of investigation, and investigation staff will only call for files in the more difficult cases and will rarely interview the civil servants concerned. An advantage of the British system is its thoroughness, but it does tend to delay. It would clearly not be possible to conduct such investigations if there were a huge increase in the numbers of complaints. The time taken by the PCA to conduct investigations is a source of dissatisfaction. The average time taken in 1992 to complete an investigation was 12 months 13 days, which was a reduction on the average time of 13 months 18 days taken in 1991 (*PCA Annual Report* 1992: 4), and a further reduction on the 14 months 25 days taken in 1990 (*PCA Annual Report* 1991: 4). One of the objectives of the present PCA is to reduce the average investigation time to nine months, and to have an average report length of ten pages (*PCA Annual Report* 1991: 49–50).

The method of working has been very much influenced by the office of the Comptroller and Auditor-General, and indicates that the PCA is seen very much as an internal administrative audit. Justice (1977: 6–7) has argued that the very thorough method of investigation is unnecessary for the more routine or simple type of case, where a telephone inquiry could often produce a change in decision and immediate redress for a complainant. It was suggested that the PCA should adopt simpler methods for some cases, reserving the 'Rolls-Royce' method for the more difficult ones. If there were more complaints, simpler methods might have to be used in the more routine cases. These might include, for example, a telephone or written inquiry to the department concerned.

The Northern Ireland Commissioner has such a procedure and operates a two-tier system. A thorough investigation takes about thirteen months, but some cases are dealt with more informally, and a telephone call or fax usually gets an immediate reply. The average time taken for these cases is six weeks (HC 182, 1991: 4, 5, 8). Even if it were not thought appropriate to have a two-tier system for the PCA, the degree of thoroughness of investigation could be varied, especially where the facts were not in dispute. In these cases the PCA should not duplicate the internal investigations carried out by the department, but should evaluate the department's performance in the light of what is good administration. A less thorough investigation in some cases would not necessarily impair the PCA's effectiveness as an administrative critic (see Gregory and Pearson 1992: 493–5).

There is no opportunity to cross-examine, and any inconsistencies in the evidence cannot be tested as they could in a court. In many cases the ombudsman can only note the inconsistencies, without passing any judgement. When this information has been obtained, the ombudsman prepares a report, conclusions and, if appropriate, recommendations as to the remedy. A draft is sent to the department, where it is checked for accuracy, and to see if the department is prepared to grant the remedy suggested where there is a finding of maladministration and injustice (*PCA Annual Report* 1991: 5).

When an investigation is completed, Section 10 requires the ombudsman to send a copy of the results report to the Member of the House of Commons who requested the investigation of the complaint. A copy has to be sent to the principal officer of the department concerned, and to the civil servants who were alleged to have taken, or authorized, the action complained of. The ombudsman has interpreted this section in such a way that he only sends the report to those required by the Act. The result of this is that publicity for the reports is patchy, as it is left to the individual MP to decide whether to publicize or not. Some do inform the press, but some do not, and even those who do usually only inform the local newspaper.

The ombudsman can report directly to Parliament, but there is no power within the Act to report directly to the complainant. It is for MPs to report to the complainants, and for them to decide whether to give the matter any publicity. The PCA's powers and duties end with the report on the case.

CASES INVESTIGATED

One of the most striking features of the statistics in relation to the PCA is the small number of complaints that are dealt with each year. Since its inception, there have never been more than 380 cases investigated per year, the highest number, 374, coming in 1968. Since 1983, the number investigated per year has never reached 200 (see *PCA Annual Reports*). The yearly average number of cases investigated in the period 1967 to 1991 was 225, and the yearly average number of complaints referred by MPs was 803 (Gregory and Pearson 1992: 471). This is in marked contrast to the estimated six to seven thousand complaints a year which were anticipated when the office was first established (Stacey 1978: 129). The number of complaints referred by MPs in 1992 was 945 (*PCA Annual Report* 1992: 4), which represented an increase on the 1991 figure of 801. The 1990 figure of 704 was an increase from the previous year's figure of 677, and is thought to have been because of the publicity surrounding the PCA's investigation on the Barlow Clowes affair, which increased general awareness of the office (*PCA Annual Report* 1990: 4). The number of referrals in 1992 was the highest since 1980, and may be partly explained by an increasing general public awareness of the role and usefulness of ombudsmen. The present ombudsman believes, however, that the increase is largely owing to increased expectations on the part of the public (*PCA Annual Report* 1992: 1).

Despite the increase, these are still small numbers. By contrast, many ombudsmen worldwide, serving far smaller populations, receive and investigate far more cases. For example, in Denmark the ombudsman receives more than two thousand complaints from a population of about five million. In Sweden the ombudsman receives about four thousand cases each year from a population of about eight million. These figures are not a reflection of higher staffing levels, the ratio of staff to cases investigated being about 1:10 for the PCA, compared to 1:60 in Denmark, 1:85 in Sweden, and 1:80 in New Zealand (see Gwyn 1982: 181).

Most complaints forwarded by MPs are rejected, only about 25 per cent of cases each year being accepted for investigation. Of the cases rejected, over 50 per cent are because the complaint does not concern administrative actions, as required by Section 5(1) of the Act. The rest are because: there is an alternative right of appeal to a tribunal; the complaint is against an authority outside the scope of the Act; the PCA uses his discretion not to investigate; or the matter refers to personnel matters, which are excluded by Schedule 3.

When cases are accepted for investigation, the complaint is likely to be upheld. Since 1983, over 40 per cent of investigations have resulted in the complaint being wholly justified, with a similar number being partly justified. In the past five years, only between 7 and 11 per cent of cases investigated have been held to be unjustified. In 1992, 54 per cent of complaints were found to be fully justified, 39 per cent partly justified, and 7 per cent not justified. This contrasts with the position in 1967, when in only 10 per cent of cases was maladministration found.

Each year, departments that have twenty or more complaints directed against them are listed in the annual reports. Perhaps not surprisingly, the Department of Social Security is always at the top of this list, followed by the Inland Revenue. Their combined share of the total referrals has accounted for over 40 per cent of all referrals in the past ten years. These departments attract the most complaints because their administration brings them into direct contact with the public. They are therefore more likely to be the subject of a complaint than those, like the Treasury, which do not have such contact, and where there is no direct and immediate personal impact.

During the past five years, the Department of Social Security has accounted for between 28 and 31 per cent of all complaints and investigations. This figure should be set against the fact that the department deals with twenty million claims per year for a variety of benefits and allowances, and the PCA has observed that the volume of complaints 'is an indicator not . . . of their maladministration so much as of their day-to-day contact with the public' (HC 129, 1991: para. 24).

A large number of these complaints relate to the administration of social security benefits, and include such matters as the incorrect stoppage of benefit, the mishandling of benefit claims, inadequate, misleading or poor advice in relation to entitlement to retirement pensions, and inefficiency and delay. One case (C534/89) concerned unwieldy and inappropriate procedures used in seeking to correct a mistake made by a doctor on an attendance allowance certificate. In this case the remedy was the introduction of revised procedures.

A matter of concern in relation to the Department of Social Security is the social fund. The social fund was set up to give loans and grants to claimants. If claimants disagree with decisions of social fund officers, they can have their case reviewed by the officer, by a colleague and finally by the social fund inspectorate. There is no right of appeal to an independent tribunal. The department has taken the view that since the social fund is separate from the department and is not its agent, the jurisdiction of the PCA does not extend to it. It so happens that the PCA has received 'virtually no complaints' about the way the social fund machinery is working (*PCA Annual Report* 1988: 9), but the Select Committee has taken up this issue with the department. However, due to the fact that there have been no complaints about the administration of the social fund, the Select Committee has decided to make no comment on the issue, but will pursue it should problems arise. This jurisdictional issue is, therefore, still unresolved (see *PCA Annual Report* 1990: 11–12).

The number of complaints relating to the Inland Revenue has accounted for between 12 and 19 per cent of all cases in the past five years. As with the Department of Social Security, this has to be set in the context of over thirty million taxpayers and over one million companies with which the Inland Revenue is concerned (HC 129, 1991: para. 26). Typical complaints include: delays, mishandling and inefficiency in dealing with fees and expenses; wrong advice given to taxpayers; errors in valuations; breach of confidentiality about a taxpayer's affairs to the taxpayer's employer. The Chairman of the Inland Revenue has expressed an intention and objective to reduce the number of cases going to the PCA, and has outlined measures to reduce the potential for complaints. These include: sending copies of a Taxpayers' Charter with tax returns; encouraging MPs to write to Treasury Ministers or himself when they cannot gain satisfaction from a local office; retaining skilled staff; expanding the use of computers (HC 129, 1991: paras 26 and 27).

The Home Office has accounted for between 4 and 5 per cent of all complaints during the past five years. Cases include delays or mishandling in relation to immigration matters, and delays and mishandling of passport applications. The ombudsman also dealt with complaints about the mishandling of enquiries about television licences. However, responsibility for the issue of television licences and for the collection of revenue was transferred from the Home Office to the BBC on 1 April 1991, under the provisions of the Broadcasting Act 1990. The BBC is not within the jurisdiction of the PCA, and therefore complaints in relation to these licences will no longer be dealt with by the PCA.

Complaints against the Department of the Environment have accounted for between 7 and 9 per cent of all cases in the past five years. These tend to involve delays in relation to, or the mishandling of, planning appeals. Other departments mentioned as having twenty or more complaints include the Department of Transport, the Department of Trade and Industry and the Department of Employment, which typically have between 4 and 5 per cent of the total share of complaints each year.

In general, the types of criticisms levelled against departments by the PCA include: assorted mistakes, errors and oversights; failure to impart information or provide an adequate explanation; the giving of inaccurate information and misleading advice; misapplication of departmental rules and instructions; peremptory or inconsiderate behaviour on the part of officials; unjustified delay; failure to treat, as far as is possible, like cases alike. A common fault is a failure by officials to consider the relevant factors in the case in question, and by departments to follow the necessary procedures to elicit the relevant information.

PRISONS OMBUDSMAN

The PCA deals with cases involving complaints from prisoners, prisons being administered by the Home Office. Prisons contracted out to the private sector are still within the PCA's jurisdiction, so that complaints from prisoners in these establishments can be investigated (*PCA Annual Report* 1992: 27–8). Complaints from prisoners have never formed a major part of the PCA's workload. In 1990 the ombudsman accepted for investigation only two complaints from prisoners out of seven received (*PCA Annual Report* 1990: 21). In 1991 only four investigations from prisoners were completed (*PCA Annual Report* 1991: 21). In 1992, fifteen complaints were received from prisoners, and two investigations were completed (*PCA Annual Report* 1992: 27–8). Concern has been expressed about these low numbers, and it has been asked whether such numbers can possibly reflect the extent of maladministration arguably causing injustice within the present prison system (see Bradley 1992: 355). Justice (1977: 20–1) felt that there were areas of prison life barely touched on by the ombudsman, and it is felt that the MP filter is a strong disincentive to prisoners.

The Home Office recently amended the rules for handling prisoners' complaints. The new complaints system, introduced by the Home Office on 15 September 1990, resulted in no obvious change in the numbers of prisoners' complaints going to the PCA (*PCA Annual Report* 1991: 21), although it is probably too early to tell whether there will be fewer complaints (*PCA Annual Report* 1992: 27).

Concerns about the low numbers of complaints to the PCA led to calls for a separate Prisons Ombudsman, and in January 1993 the Home Secretary announced that he would be appointing such an ombudsman, to consider grievances from prisoners who have failed to obtain satisfaction from the present internal complaints system. The Prisons Ombudsman will be a final and independent point of appeal for individual prisoners, and will have a wide remit, including disciplinary issues. Unlike the PCA, the Prisons Ombudsman will be able to consider the merits of cases as well as the procedures involved. She or he has no statutory powers, but will make recommendations to the chief executive of the Prison Service, and the Home Secretary as necessary, and will publish an annual report.

This new ombudsman will not affect the right of prisoners to approach the PCA, through an MP, where the matter is one of alleged maladministration. It is too early to evaluate the work of the Prisons Ombudsman, or to assess the effect on the work of the PCA, but in view of the concerns expressed above the appointment is to be welcomed.

STAFFING

The PCA's office has a large staff in relation to the number of investigations per year. This is a result of the 'Rolls Royce' character of the investigations, which involves high-level reviews. In 1992 there was a staff of thirty-two and a half for Parliamentary Commissioner work, and thirty for Health Service Commissioner work. In addition there were thirty-three and a half support staff for both branches of the office. The entire investigations staff in the office is on secondment from government departments or the health service, normally for three years. The majority of the commissioners themselves, since 1967, have been former civil servants, although some have been lawyers. This leads to the idea that the best people to investigate civil servants are civil servants, because they have specialized administrative expertise which will make it easier for them to detect failings. This is very much the same argument as that made for police officers investigating complaints against the police.

It can be argued that there is a need to make the office independent of the civil service. There could be a danger that, because the ombudsman has a civil service background and all the staff are civil servants, the public may feel there is some bias towards the civil service view. There could be a lack of confidence if the investigating institution is not seen to be fully independent of the department concerned. It would therefore be advantageous if the staff were not all on secondment from the various government departments being investigated.

However, one of the problems of making permanent, rather than seconded, appointments is that there is no permanent career structure within the PCA's office. The use of civil servants can be seen as an advantage, as they are aware of civil service practices, and the charge of bias is answered by the fact that an officer does not investigate his or her previous department. Gwyn (1982) believes that civil servants have proved to be very careful, thorough and unbiased investigators, with considerable knowledge of administrative practices and behaviour, and concludes that it is 'difficult to find outsiders with better qualifications' (p. 180). It is also felt that these staff return to their departments with a more informed outlook, and a better idea of what constitutes good administrative practice, which can have nothing but benefit for their departmental work.

However, if the ombudsman is to be seen to be genuinely independent, then perhaps civil servants, although not becoming ineligible, should not dominate the appointments. The advantage of civil servants is that they know how the system works, but they are also imbued with Whitehall ways. There are obvious advantages in appointing some civil servants, but there should also be appointments from outside the civil service. Lessons could be learnt from the local government ombudsmen, whose staff are drawn from a variety of backgrounds, including local government. Perhaps the PCA could make seconded appointments from local government.

The PCA does not have a legal adviser on the staff and in the past took advice from the Treasury Solicitor or from the legal advisers of the departments under investigation. In recent years the PCA has frequently taken independent legal advice, but there is an argument for having a staff legal adviser, and one not on secondment from the civil service.

ACCESS TO THE PCA

The Whyatt Committee (Justice 1961: 75–6) recommended that access to the PCA should be through MPs and also through peers, although this latter recommendation was never taken up. The provision for access was seen as experimental, and it was proposed that it should be reviewed after five years.

The argument for restricting access in this way was that if there were direct access in a country with over fifty-five million people, the ombudsman would be swamped with cases. However, the number of cases anticipated was greatly overestimated. It was expected that there would be between six and seven thousand complaints a year (see Stacey 1978: 129), but the largest number ever received in a year was 1,259 in 1978. Of these, most were rejected, and the number actually investigated in that year was 341. The numbers of complaints referred to the PCA in recent years are as follows:

Year	Number
1992	945
1991	801
1990	704
1989	677
1988	701
1987	677
1986	719

Although the numbers of complaints are beginning to increase, they are still well below those anticipated. If the reason for the member filter was to prevent 'swamping', it has proved too successful.

There was also a belief that the majority of MPs wanted the member filter. Such an attitude is not uncommon. In Australia the ombudsman was originally viewed with suspicion by members, who feared that the office would usurp their role, weaken their political leverage with constituents and dent their profile (Wiltshire 1988: 146). Certainly, when the Bill was being debated in Parliament, stress was laid on the ombudsman's potential to assist backbench MPs and on the PCA's status as a servant of the House (HC Deb., Vol. 734). Direct access was seen as undermining the position of

MPs in relation to the public. There is no doubt that indirect access involved a shift in philosophy, emphasizing the role of the ombudsman as a means of enhancing the role of backbenchers and making the office very much a matter for Parliamentary control (Gregory and Hutchesson 1975: 91). It had become a 'parliamentary' rather than a 'public' institution (Drewry and Harlow 1990: 748), an aid to members of the legislature in their role as a check on the executive.

The member filter has attracted criticism. The report by Justice (1977: 17–18) highlighted the fact that the ombudsman was little used, and saw the MP filter as partly to blame for this. It recommended the removal of the MP filter. In 1978, a new procedure was introduced for dealing with direct complaints. If the complaint is clearly outside the PCA's jurisdiction then the complainant is informed of this. The complainant would similarly be informed if the problem seemed more suitable for the MP to handle. If, however, it seems that an investigation by the PCA would be appropriate, the PCA writes to the complainant, offering to send it to an MP and saying that she or he is prepared to start an investigation should the member wish him or her to do so. If the complainant decides to proceed, he or she is not required to complain again from the beginning. The MP can either take up the complaint on the complainant's behalf or consent to the ombudsman's proceeding direct to an investigation. There are very few cases (rarely more than ten) that are investigated under this procedure each year and, of course, it is still necessary under the procedure for an MP to agree that the complaint be dealt with by the PCA (Justice 1988: 89). In fact, in a recent annual report, the ombudsman admits that the advice given to direct complainants, where the matter is within the PCA's jurisdiction, is to use the MP route. It is then a matter for the MP whether to refer the case to the ombudsman or to pursue it in some other way (*PCA Annual Report* 1991: 30).

There seems to be little justification for the member filter. Rowat (1985: 135) believes that this is a serious limitation on the ombudsman's powers, which arose from the unnecessarily conservative proposals of the Whyatt Report. The reasons for the member filter was to reduce the load on the ombudsman in such a large country, and to make the scheme more palatable to members who feared loss of contact with their constituents. He concludes that 'many people . . . feel that this is an undesirable restriction . . . because many complainants will not wish to take their case to a partisan politician, and he will be an extra screen between them and the administration' (p. 135).

A right to complain to an MP does not provide sufficient safeguards for complainants. There are the problems of partiality and suitability, and also of party affiliation. In addition, MPs have other work to do. In 1973 it was shown that MPs 'use the office very sparingly indeed by comparison with the frequency with which they employ the established techniques for helping constituents' (Gregory and Alexander 1973: 48). Recent research draws a similar conclusion. Thus it was found that, in 1986, 263 MPs (40.5 per cent) referred no complaints to the PCA, and only 85 MPs (13 per cent) referred three or more complaints. Many MPs do not hold the office in high esteem, and some were unaware of the scope and functions of the office (see Drewry and Harlow 1990).

In the world ombudsman community only the French Mediateur joins the PCA in resisting direct access. The Health Service Commissioner and the Local Government Ombudsman have direct access, and this makes the member filter even more anomalous. Justice (1988: 90) has once more recommended that the 1967 Act should be amended to provide direct access. This would enable the ombudsman to project himself to the public in a more positive way. Cecil Clothier had favoured a compromise position. A complainant must first approach an MP to take up the grievance with the department, but if he or she were then dissatisfied with the progress being made, there should be a right to refer the case directly to the PCA (*PCA Annual Report* 1983: para. 7). Justice (1988: 89) believes that a more vigorous approach is needed, and that there is 'an urgent need for missionary work by the PCA'. Despite the fears of MPs that it would reduce their surgery work, public interest makes such a change necessary.

This view is not shared by the Select Committee on the PCA. In its report in 1990–1 it endorsed the observations made by the Select Committee in 1978: that the filter worked to the advantage of the complainant because the problem could be resolved quickly by an MP; that it was advantageous to members because they were kept in touch with constituency problems; and that the ombudsman gained because complaints were referred only where the member was unable to reach a solution. They saw no reason for abolishing the member filter, but recommended more publicity for MPs about the commissioner's work (HC 129, 1991: paras 29, 30). The commissioner took up the Select Committee's suggestion, and wrote personally to every MP enclosing a revised and reissued guidance leaflet on his role and functions (HC 368, 1991: para. 10).

An alternative approach is suggested by Rawlings (1986a). He acknowledges the increasing workload of MPs in grievance resolution, and recognizes that, for many people, the MP is a likely port of call for those with grievances, particularly in relation to problems involving maladministration or general personal difficulties (p. 122). He believes that the MP filter should continue, so that members can handle the routine cases and the ombudsman can be brought in for the more difficult ones (p. 138). But he would like to see procedures established to encourage members to report to the Select Committee cases or patterns of cases which suggest serious or recurring instances of maladministration. The Select Committee would be empowered to identify problem areas by recording and tracking complaints, to summon and question civil servants, and to direct the PCA to investigate. Such a proposal would facilitate a broad, systematic and responsive use of the oversight function of the Parliamentary redress of grievance (p. 139).

Such a system would necessitate more publicity for the work of the PCA, addressed to MPs, and a greater willingness on the part of MPs to refer cases (see Drewry and Harlow 1990). The commissioner at the time of writing, William Reid, has no objection to direct access, and has told the Select Committee (HC 650, 1993: 10) that it is 'potentially disadvantageous' for complainants to have to approach the PCA through an MP. Some members of the committee, however, are concerned that MPs might lose contact with constituency problems if there were direct access.

INITIATING COMPLAINTS

The complaint can be made by an individual or body of persons, whether incorporated or not, which means that companies, partnerships, trustees, amenity groups or interest groups can have their complaints investigated. It is also possible for a complaint to be made on behalf of another person. Section 6(2) of the 1967 Act provides for a complaint to be made by the personal representative of a deceased, or by a member of the family or other suitable representative where a person is for any reason unable to act for him or herself. In all other cases, the person aggrieved must make the complaint. A complaint is treated as made by a person if it is made by an employee or agent of that person. Thus complaints have been accepted from solicitors on behalf of clients, and from other professionals and professional bodies.

What Section 6(2) does prevent is the making of complaints on behalf of others where there is no question of there being an agency, and where there are no particular links between the complainant and the person aggrieved. The PCA has ruled that there cannot be acceptance of a complaint from a person 'who claims to have sustained injustice in consequence of action taken in relation to another person' (HC 385, 1969: para. 15). This ruling is interesting in view of the Barlow Clowes case, where it was the government's contention that the PCA should not be investigating cases where the complainants had no direct relationship with the relevant government department. Nevertheless, the PCA felt that he had jurisdiction in this case.

This section also prevents the ombudsman investigating on his or her own initiative, where there is no person aggrieved who is prepared to make a complaint. In this respect, it is interesting to compare the PCA with the Comptroller and Auditor General (on whom the office was modelled), who does not investigate on the basis of complaints, but on his or her own initiative in the course of carrying out the functions of auditor. The PCA can only act upon a complaint, and there is no power to act where there is a suspicion that there is something amiss. Indeed, in the absence of a written complaint from a member of the public, an MP cannot act on his or her own initiative and request the PCA to investigate an issue.

Most ombudsmen worldwide are able to conduct investigations on their own initiative. The Swedish ombudsman has a power to inspect administrative transactions, and thus acts as a permanent commission on administrative procedure and efficiency. The nearest equivalents in the UK are the National Audit Office for central government and the Audit Commission for local government, but their roles are very different from that of the ombudsmen. The Austrian ombudsman is entitled to investigate suspected grievances, and the Australian Commonwealth ombudsman has these powers, although they are rarely exercised. Haller's (1988: 40) survey indicated that the only ombudsmen not to have this power are the British, the French, the German Federal Petitions Committee, and those of Liechtenstein and the City of Zurich. There seems little justification for denying these powers to the British ombudsmen, and a reason for giving such powers is to protect the interests of those who are too weak and oppressed to protect their own.

In 1978 the Select Committee recommended that if the PCA had reason to believe that a particular section of a department was not dealing properly with its business, then, subject to the approval of the Select Committee, the PCA ought to have power to carry out a systematic investigation of it. The shortcomings in the department would come to light as a result of individual complaints, and the PCA should be empowered to identify the causes of the problem and make recommendations for improvements (HC 615, 1978).

This proposal was rejected by the government, on the grounds that such additional powers were not necessary and would detract the PCA from the task of investigating individual complaints (Government Observations 1979). Despite the government's view, there seems little justification for this exclusion, and it has been said that the 'arguments against giving an Ombudsman these powers are specious in the extreme' (Wiltshire 1988: 155). There are cases where one or more complaints about a department may alert the PCA to the fact that there is something amiss in that area of the department's work, or the PCA may wish to review the way a department deals with a class or category of work, as a result of complaints in that area.

Where ombudsmen do have this power, it appears that it is sparingly used. However, it can have important consequences for a wide range of people. For example, in New Zealand, where the ombudsman's role is not limited to resolving individual complaints, there were a number of complaints from Telecom subscribers about Telecom's standard terms of contract. The New Zealand ombudsman therefore initiated her own investigation into the reasonableness of the standard telephone subscribers contract (Taggart 1990: 14).

The Select Committee was not suggesting that the PCA should have the general remit of inspecting the administrative efficiency of departments, a task that would clearly be beyond the resources of the office. However, the limited recommendation made by the Select Committee would have advantages, and its adoption has been recommended by Justice (1988: 92). William Reid does not want such a power, however, on the grounds that if he suspected that there was something that needed investigating, he could draw this to the attention of an MP. During his term of office he has never done so (HC 650, 1993: 17).

PUBLICITY

One of the weaknesses of the Parliamentary ombudsman is that few people take complaints to him. As far back as 1978 it was concluded that the PCA was 'by far the least used, in terms of population, of any of the Ombudsmen . . . surveyed' (Stacey 1978: 170). Recent figures (see Table 2) show that this is still the case, with only a small number of complaints forwarded to the commissioner each year, and with only a small number of cases actually investigated.

There was an increase in 1990 in the number of complaints received, mainly, it is thought, on account of the publicity received from the Barlow Clowes investigation. There was a further increase in 1991, the figure of 801 representing a 13.7 per cent increase on the previous year, and in 1992 the numbers increased to 945. The majority of complaints (over 75 per cent each year) are rejected by the commissioner, which casts doubt on one of the arguments for having the member filter, namely that only those cases where the PCA has jurisdiction will be referred.

In their report in 1977, Justice drew attention to the underutilization of the PCA. In the UK, with a population of fifty-five million, only 252 cases were investigated in 1974. In contrast, Sweden, with a population of eight million, had 2,368 cases investigated in the same year. In New Zealand, with

Table 2 Numbers of complaints

Year	Complaints received	Cases investigated	Cases discontinued
1992	945	190	6
1991	801	183	6
1990	704	177	12
1989	677	126	11
1988	701	120	8

Source: PCA Annual Reports

a population of three million, 414 cases were investigated. One conclusion from this is that too few people know of the existence of the PCA (Justice 1977: 4). It seems that little has changed since then, and in 1988 Justice still thought that it was a matter of concern that 'such a comparatively small number of people seek the help of the PCA', and urged greater publicity for the office (Justice 1988: 84).

The low number of complaints is partly because of inadequate publicity, one of the problems being that very few members of the public know about the work of the office, or the identity of the post-holder. The Act itself does not envisage a direct relationship with the public, as access is through MPs. However, it is still possible and desirable to publicize the office. The French Mediateur does not have direct access, but nevertheless is very publicity conscious. More could be done by the Parliamentary Commissioner in the area of publicity.

The 1967 Act requires little in the way of publicity. Section 10(4) provides that the ombudsman shall make an annual report to Parliament on the performance of his or her functions and 'may from time to time lay before each House of Parliament such other reports with respect to those functions as he thinks fit'. Reports made by the ombudsman to Parliament are rarely debated in full. They do not command a high priority on the legislative timetable (Wiltshire 1988: 147).

If, after he or she makes a report on an investigation, it appears to the ombudsman that the injustice caused to the complainant has not been, or will not be, remedied, a special report may be made to Parliament (Section 10(3)). No such report has ever been made. This may be because no such action has been necessary, as the Select Committee usually lends support to the ombudsman when a department is reluctant to implement the proposals.

Since August 1972 the ombudsman has published results reports in quarterly volumes. The majority are anonymized, omitting the names of complainants and MPs. One way of securing more publicity for the PCA would be to send a copy of each of these reports to the press, or to allow the reports to be scrutinized by journalists, unless a complainant or MP objected to publicity on the grounds of confidentiality. This is done in Scandinavia. It has been suggested that the ombudsman is prevented from doing this because Section 11(2) prevents the disclosure of information obtained during the course of investigation except for the purposes of the investigation and of any report. If this is the case, then the remedy is to amend the Act.

Another way of ensuring publicity is for the ombudsman to issue more results reports as individual reports to Parliament under Section 10(4), as was done in the Barlow Clowes case and the Sachsenhausen case. These reports have a bigger impact and receive more attention in the press. The quarterly volumes of results reports could be made more accessible. One improvement here is that, from 1991, the quarterly report includes abbreviated accounts, as well as full texts, of a selection of cases. When the quarterly reports are published, the press receives a press handout pointing to the reports of special interest. However, there is still room for improvement. There could be a systematic discussion of the trends of cases, of the suggested improvements in administration and of the impact that the reports are having on the departments. Justice (1988: 104) suggests that it would be a good idea to have a digest of cases, as at present the material is scattered throughout the annual reports, the quarterly selected cases reports and unpublished reports.

This lack of publicity lends support to the conclusion that the ombudsman sees his role 'to be more one of providing an internal administrative audit than of acting as a ready channel for uncovering and investigating citizens' grievances' (Stacey 1978: 148). However, if the office is to be effective in providing an independent investigating service, more must be done to publicize the office. The French Mediateur has issued a popular brochure, and has regional visits and meetings. The Danish ombudsman meets the press every week, and has distributed 200,000 copies of a brochure describing his work to citizens. The Commonwealth ombudsman in Australia advertised his existence on milk bottle tops, by an arrangement with the milk suppliers. The Austrian ombudsman has a prime-time television slot advertising his function and explaining cases he has recently resolved. In Britain, by contrast, the PCA is seen very much as an adjunct to Parliament rather than directly as a citizen's defender.

The problem of low visibility may also have something to do with the kind of people who are appointed as PCAs. Generally, they have not regarded publicity for the office as a high priority, nor have they seemed to be unduly alarmed at the low number of complaints. There may be signs that this is changing. The Select Committee has recognized that publicity and awareness are important to the functioning of the office, and the PCA has recently written personally to every MP enclosing the new revised leaflet on his role and functions. The PCA has, however, noted that the anonymity of complainants in reports has militated against greater publicity in individual cases (HC 368, 1991: para. 10). The ombudsman has also appeared on television and radio and contributed to professional journals. Revised leaflets on the ombudsman were introduced in 1991, and over 160,000 of these were distributed by way of public libraries and Citizens Advice Bureaux. In addition, the explanatory video on the role of the PCA is being updated (*PCA Annual Report* 1991: 3).

The problem of publicity is closely related to that of access. Stacey, writing in 1978, identified that a great weakness of the Parliamentary Commissioner system was that so few people took their complaints to him (p. 170). As well as poor publicity, Stacey attributed this to the fact that complainants could not complain directly. More people had complained directly than had gone through their MPs, and these had had to be rejected. Little has changed since Stacey was writing. Without direct access, more publicity could lead to frustration. More publicity may lead complainants to request MPs to forward their cases to the ombudsman, but the decision to do so rests with the MP. Direct access would make the office more accessible to the general public, and would make any publicity or missionary work by the PCA more useful.

ROLE OF SELECT COMMITTEE

The Select Committee on the Parliamentary Commissioner for Administration was set up in April 1967 to examine the reports laid before the House by the PCA, and any matters in connection with them. It began work in November 1967. It is appointed under Standing Order Number 126 and examines the reports of the Parliamentary Commissioner for Administration, the Health Service Commissioner and the Northern Ireland Commissioner. The Committee has power to send for persons, papers and records, to sit notwithstanding any adjournment of the House, to adjourn from place to place and to report from time to time. It can also appoint persons with technical knowledge, either to supply information which is not readily available or to elucidate matters of complexity. Its composition is related to party composition in the House of Commons, and its Chair is a member of the Opposition. At the time of writing there are nine members, five Conservative and four Labour.

The establishment of the Select Committee firmly places the ombudsman in the Parliamentary context. The ombudsman is responsible to and reports to Parliament, and the Select Committee examines these reports, and generally oversees how the ombudsman is performing his or her role. It obtains its information from the PCA's annual reports, quarterly reports and special individual reports. When it receives this information, it decides which civil servants to summon for examination of issues contained in them. The ombudsman is present during these examinations, and gives evidence.

It is generally believed that the appointment of the Select Committee has been very valuable, and that it has enhanced the effectiveness of the ombudsman. It was left largely to establish its own role, and its concerns have been the extent to which the ombudsman's recommendations are being implemented in the departments and the effects of the investigations on administration within the departments. It seems that the Select Committee has given sufficient support to the ombudsman when departments have raised difficulties about implementing recommendations. An early success was in 1975, when the government was persuaded to change the law to allow the Inland Revenue to pay interest on tax which had been overpaid after there had been some delay in its repayment.

The Committee does not reinvestigate cases, but takes the commissioner's reports as they stand. If a department does not remedy a justified grievance, it would be the duty of the Select Committee to report that fact to the House of Commons. But the fact that there is this authority, and that the PCA commands the support of the Select Committee, means that departments are reluctant to ignore the PCA's recommendations and the Select Committee has been successful in bringing pressure to bear on departments (see Justice 1988: 87). The Committee has also taken the view that, where the ombudsman has found the faulty operation of an administrative system, it could examine the department to see what steps had been taken to identify and remedy the defects.

The Select Committee has addressed the issue of whether the ombudsman's powers of investigation should be strengthened or jurisdiction widened. In general, there has been a tendency to favour widening jurisdiction and strengthening his or her position in investigations. It has encouraged the ombudsman to take a broad view of the concept of maladministration, but has had little success in persuading the government to broaden jurisdiction, and its recommendations in the *Review of Access and Jurisdiction* (HC 615, 1978) were largely ignored. A recent success, however, was the recommendation made in 1984 that over fifty non-departmental public bodies should be included within the ombudsman's jurisdiction (HC 619, 1984). This recommendation was substantially implemented by the Parliamentary and Health Service Commissioners Act 1987. At the time of writing the Select Committee is conducting a wide-ranging enquiry into the powers, work and jurisdiction of the ombudsman (HC 650, 1993).

THE CITIZEN'S CHARTER

In 1991, the government published its White Paper on The Citizen's Charter the purpose of which is to improve the quality of public services and make them more responsive to their users. There are references throughout the Citizen's Charter to departmental charters, which have started to emerge, and it contains a statement of principles on what the citizen is entitled to expect from public services. One would have thought that the value of the ombudsman would have been stressed in the Charter, but in all its fifty-one pages there is only a brief recognition of the Health Service Commissioner's (HSC) role in hospital complaints, and a brief reference to the HSC and PCA in providing an external remedy should the internal procedures fail (see Bradley 1992: 356). In a study of the Charter, Barron and Scott (1992: 531) discuss the empowering of citizens by extending complaints mechanisms, but do not once mention the ombudsman.

Despite this oversight by the government, the PCA recognized that the Charter could have implications for his work, and in 1991 the Select Committee undertook a brief inquiry into its possible implications (HC 158, 1992). In relation to the departmental charters, the PCA said in evidence to the Select Committee that these would help to provide a standard by which to measure the maladministration alleged. However, he added that he was still unfettered in his discretion to determine whether or not maladministration has taken place. In this way the PCA's investigations can assist the Citizen's Charter Unit to monitor implementation within departments, and provide some independent validation of performance against standards.

The Charter programme itself will assist the work of the Parliamentary Commissioner. For example, many cases that come before the PCA have been preceded by a complaint to the public body concerned, which has not been responded to satisfactorily. As the Charter attaches importance to the effectiveness of internal complaints procedures in the public service, this may result in these complaints being satisfactorily resolved at departmental level. Where standards have fallen and complaints are justified, the Charter states that there should be an apology and redress where appropriate. As this is what the PCA seeks when a complaint is justified, this again could result in a satisfactory outcome at departmental level, without recourse to the ombudsman.

In addition, the internal complaints procedures themselves, recommended in the Charter, can help to serve some of the same purposes as the PCA. The Charter emphasizes that where complaints highlight problems, 'lessons must be learnt so that mistakes are not repeated' (White Paper 1991: 5). Complaints procedures are therefore to be central to the work of the department. These improvements in internal complaints procedures would enable more citizens' grievances to be settled before they reached the ombudsman. Of course, no matter how effective internal procedures are, it is still essential to retain an external, impartial investigator, so the ombudsman's role would not be diminished.

One area of concern for the Select Committee was in relation to lay adjudicators (HC 158, 1992: paras 8 and 9). The Citizen's Charter sees these as providing external routes for dissatisfied complainants. The Select Committee was concerned that this proposal could undermine the ombudsman's role. The PCA provides a thorough and independent external route for complainants, and it would be wrong if lay adjudicators could pre-empt the PCA's decision, or undermine the right to complain to him or her. It was therefore recommended that the role of lay adjudicators should be advisory, and that where a speedy resolution to a grievance appeared unlikely, complainants should be referred to the PCA (para. 9). The Local Government Ombudsman agreed with the Select Committee on this point (*CLA Annual Report* 1991–2: 6), and it seems likely that this recommendation will be heeded.

The Charter makes no proposals to change the powers or jurisdiction of the PCA. However, one of the key principles of the Charter is 'well sign-posted avenues for complaint . . . with some means of independent review wherever possible' (White Paper 1991: 6). The Select Committee has seen this commitment as perhaps indicating a willingness by the government to reconsider existing limitations on the jurisdiction of the ombudsman, and a feeling that the government may be coming around to its own view that all decisions of civil servants within departments, involving maladministration, should be within jurisdiction, unless there is a constitutional principle which dictates otherwise (HC 158, 1992: para. 13).

Another concern of the Select Committee is that the sheer variety of complaints mechanisms should not divert attention away from the PCA's role. It therefore recommends that leaflets about complaints should mention the PCA (HC 158, 1992: para. 14). However, the problem of raising awareness, as has already been mentioned, is that this raises the question of access, with the member filter being seen as an obstruction. The present PCA recognizes the disadvantages of the member filter, particularly when the system is compared with foreign jurisdictions and the Local Government Ombudsman. Notwithstanding this, the Select Committee believes that the advantages of the filter outweigh its disadvantages, and is not prepared to recommend a change in this area (HC 158, 1992: para. 15).

The conclusion reached by the Select Committee on the implications of the Citizen's Charter for the work of the PCA is that the Charter programme provides an opportunity to raise standards in public services, and it is hoped that this will reduce the number of grievances that might come to the ombudsman. The standards set out in individual charters should also provide the ombudsman with some, but not the only, benchmarks against which it can be determined whether there has been maladministration (HC 158, 1992: para. 16). However, they will not be the *determinant* of what constitutes maladministration, and that remains for the ombudsman to decide, taking into account all the circumstances in each individual case (*PCA Annual Report* 1991: 3).

CONCLUSIONS

The ombudsman principle, according to a previous PCA, Anthony Barrowclough, is that 'citizens with grievances concerning the administrative actions of government departments or public bodies are entitled to an *independent* investigation and appraisal of the justification . . . for their complaints' (*PCA Annual Report* 1988: 1). How far the PCA conforms to this principle is a matter of concern.

In 1977, Justice concluded that although the institution of Parliamentary

Commissioner for Administration had worked well, it had done so only 'within a very restricted frame of reference' (Justice 1977: 1). As an institution it was limited in scope and effectiveness, compared to similar institutions in other common law countries, and on the continent. Little has changed since 1977, and although Justice has recently concluded that 'the introduction of the Ombudsman has improved the position of the citizen *vis-à-vis* the administrator' (Justice 1988: 84), there is still much concern that it is not widely known to the public, is considerably underutilized and is far from accessible. One improvement would be to have direct access.

Another way of tackling the problem of underutilization is to place more emphasis on publicity, as the public do not understand what the ombudsman scheme is about (see Bradley 1992: 355). A recent improvement was the inclusion in the 1991 annual report of photographs of the present ombudsman and his predecessors, which helps to make the office more accessible, although this was not repeated in the 1992 annual report. The press could play a greater role: they should be informed of the results of investigations, and more use should be made of press conferences. Annual and quarterly reports should be more informative, and more effort should be taken to publicize the work of the office, both in relation to the general public and in relation to MPs. There are also problems relating to jurisdiction, as it is unsatisfactory that any public body is excluded unless overwhelming reasons can be shown to the contrary. Apart from being inequitable, such a patchwork jurisdiction must lead to confusion in the minds of citizens.

As the PCA was set up as an adjunct to Parliament, it is perhaps within that context that the impact of the office ought to be examined. The Whyatt Report (Justice 1961) took a narrow, grievance-redressing view of the PCA's function, and did not even consider the objective of identifying and eradicating administrative inefficiency (see Rawlings 1986a: 124). Despite this, it has become accepted that part of the ombudsman's role is to encourage public officials to maintain acceptable standards of good administration (see Justice 1988: 86). This is not out of line with ombudsmen worldwide, Haller's (1988: 35–6) recent survey finding that forty-one out of forty-three ombudsmen canvassed claimed to wish to improve administrative practice, and the same number also included proposals for improving legislation and administrative rules in the catalogue of their functions.

How far the PCA has gone in relation to this objective is questionable. Justice floated the idea of establishing a code of principles of good administration (Justice 1988: 20), but the then PCA, Cecil Clothier, was opposed to a code, fearing that such principles might become a cause of undesirable bureaucratic rigidity. The present ombudsman's view is that he is not opposed to such codes, but that it is not his role to draw these up, and that this should be left to departments. This seems to be an unnecessarily conservative view, and Justice has recommended that the best person to draw up codes of principles of good administration would be the Parliamentary Commissioner (Justice 1988: 23). The Local Government Ombudsman has begun work on drawing up such a code for local government.

The attitude of the Parliamentary Commissioners, in relation to these codes, seems to indicate that they emphasize the grievance resolution aspect of the office, rather than that of improving administrative practice. Since the function of the office is to provide independent assessment and criticism of the operation of the administration, the PCA ought clearly to be directed to making a contribution towards improved administration. Indeed, some would argue that this should be their primary role. Harlow (1978: 450–3), for example, stresses that the PCA's objective should be to scrutinize the administrative process. She is more concerned with quality, rather than quantity, and admits that the ombudsman's procedure is not appropriate for handling large numbers of cases. She sees the individual complaint as primarily a mechanism that draws attention to more general administrative deficiencies.

The impact of the PCA in improving administration is mixed. There is no direct requirement for the PCA to make a contribution to improved administration, but this is not to say that the existence of the office has not produced improvements. A reading of the reports indicates that improvements in administration have been forthcoming, but the circumstances in which these occur are unpredictable. There is no evidence that the PCA looks at the adequacy of procedures and follows up claims of improvements by departments. At present it seems that the PCA is neither achieving a large quantity of complaints, and thereby fulfilling the grievance-redress role, nor taking a stand against poor administrative practice in general. However, in the PCA's management plan this problem of improving procedures is addressed. It is recognized that an important aspect of the ombudsman's work is the knowledge that procedures will be improved to benefit others. The PCA has therefore made it a priority to meet with heads of government departments and executive agencies, and to contribute to seminars and conferences. In this way, the ombudsman's work can help to improve the quality of public services (*PCA Annual Report* 1991: 49).

In conclusion, it appears that the PCA has been a qualified success, but is less effective than other ombudsman systems. To its credit, the office has brought about improvements in administrative practice and policy, and brought redress to hundreds of complaints, without damaging civil service morale or significantly increasing departmental workloads (see Gregory and Pearson 1992: 471). However, the feeling is that it has not reached its full potential, as the low number of referrals by MPs indicates, and a general conclusion seems to be that the office is 'capable of better things' (see Drewry and Harlow 1990).

THE HEALTH SERVICE COMMISSIONER

INTRODUCTION

When the Parliamentary Commissioner Bill was being debated in Parliament in 1966 and 1967, it was strongly criticized because National Health Service hospitals were excluded from jurisdiction by Schedule 3. There were attempts to amend this provision, and in fact the government was defeated at committee stage on this, but the exclusionary provision was restored at report stage. Despite a promise to look again at this issue the government resisted pressure in the House of Lords to reinstate the amendment that would allow the investigation of complaints about National Health Service hospitals.

One of the reasons for including hospitals in the PCA's remit was the unsatisfactory procedures for complaints that existed in hospitals at the time. Despite the fact that hospitals were administered by the regional health authorities and the (then) Department of Health and Social Security, there was no standard procedure or code of practice for dealing with complaints made by inpatients and outpatients of hospitals. Ministerial guidance had been issued in 1966 (Memorandum HM(66)15, 7 March 1966) recommending a procedure for dealing with complaints not involving serious disciplinary charges against staff or court proceedings. The memorandum containing the guidance had been supplemented by a letter in the same year, drawing attention to the need for hospitals to ensure that investigations into complaints were independent, and that no one connected with the substance of the complaint should be involved in the investigation.

There were a number of proposals to improve the position in relation to hospital complaints in the years following the passing of the Parliamentary Commissioner Act 1967. In July 1968 the Select Committee on the Parliamentary Commissioner for Administration reported to the House of Commons that, in its view, the commissioner should be empowered to look at complaints about hospitals (HC 350, 1968: para. 37). At the same time the Minister of Health published a discussion document on the Health Service (Ministry of Health 1968), which included a suggestion that the Parliamentary commissioner's jurisdiction should be extended to include hospitals, or that there should be the appointment of a separate Health Service Commissioner. The proposals in the paper on reorganization of the health service were criticized, and a revised series of proposals were published in June 1970.

Many voluntary organizations were in favour of an ombudsman (see Robb 1967) but doctors' organizations were generally critical. However, at about this time there was a series of reports into allegations of ill-treatment of patients in psychiatric hospitals, one of which recommended that a 'Health Service Commissioner, given the widest possible powers, should be appointed urgently to meet public anxiety about the investigation of complaints in the health service' (Farleigh Report 1971: 29).

In February 1972 it was announced that the government intended to set up Health Service Commissioners, and the proposals were implemented by the National Health Service (Scotland) Act 1972 and the National Health Service Reorganisation Act 1973. The Acts provide for separate Health Service Commissioners for England, Wales and Scotland. However, it was decided that these roles should be filled by the Parliamentary ombudsman, the reason being that the volume of complaints to the Parliamentary ombudsman had not proved to be as great as expected, and he therefore had spare capacity to take on these additional complaints. He began to receive these complaints in 1973.

THE SCHEME

The office of the Health Service Commissioner (HSC) was created by Part III of the National Health Services Reorganisation Act 1973, which was amended by the National Health Service Act 1977, Part V. Section 106 of the 1977 Act provides that the commissioner be appointed by the Crown, and holds office during good behaviour, retiring at the age of sixty-five. She or he can be relieved of office by request, but otherwise removal can only take place on addresses from both Houses of Parliament. The salary of the

HSC is charged on the Consolidated Fund (Section 107(8)), and where a person holds both the offices of PCA and HSC, there is only entitlement to the PCA's salary (Section 107(5)).

The HSC is empowered to investigate bodies that are listed in Section 109 of the 1977 Act, and are: regional, district and special health authorities; the former family practitioner committees, now the family health services authorities; and certain other bodies, such as the Mental Health Act Commission and the Dental Practice Board. National Health Service Trusts, which were created by the National Health Service and Community Care Act 1990, are also within jurisdiction, and, like other National Health Service hospitals, they are subject to the Hospital Complaints Procedure Act 1985.

JURISDICTION

As is the case with the Parliamentary ombudsman, there are certain areas of activity that are excluded from the scheme. Section 116(2) (b) of the 1977 Act prevents the HSC from investigating complaints about services provided by family doctors, dentists, opticians and pharmacists. The practitioners who provide these services are independent, having contracts with local family health services authorities to provide services in the particular area. Complaints about these services must be made to the local family health services authority, which can try to settle the matter informally or investigate the complaint under a formal procedure. The procedure is designed to find out whether the practitioner's terms of contract have been broken, and there is a right of appeal from the decision to the Secretary of State for Health.

Section 116(2) (a) provides that the ombudsman may not investigate those matters listed in Part II of Schedule 13 of the Act. There are five such matters listed in the schedule, and these will be examined in turn.

Clinical decisions (para. 19(1)). One of the most important exclusions is that relating to clinical judgement. The schedule states that action 'taken in connection with the diagnosis of illness or the care or treatment of a patient, being action which, in the opinion of the Commissioner in question, was taken solely in consequence of the exercise of clinical judgement, whether formed by the person taking the action or any other person' is excluded from jurisdiction. Thus complaints about action taken solely as a result of a clinical judgement in the provision of diagnosis, care or treatment, including wrong diagnosis and treatment, cannot be investigated, despite any harm that may befall the patient. It is a wide exclusion, covering doctors, nurses and paramedics.

This exclusion, which was included in the Act at the insistence of the British Medical Association, has been the subject of much controversy. It is often argued that jurisdiction should be expanded to cover clinical judge-ment, and that the effectiveness of the HSC is reduced by this limitation. From the beginning, by far the largest category of complaints rejected by the HSC concerned those relating to clinical judgement. In 1975, about one-sixth of cases were rejected as being outside jurisdiction because they were complaints about the diagnosis or treatment of patients solely con-cerned with the exercise of clinical judgement by medical staff (HC 282, 1976: para. 4). Since that date, the numbers of rejections on this ground have fluctuated from 40 per cent of all rejections in 1978, to 16 per cent in 1989. In 1991–3, over one-fifth of all rejected grievances have been concerned with clinical judgement.

The position in relation to complaints about clinical matters may have been alleviated to some extent by the introduction of the clinical complaints procedure in 1981. This was introduced to deal with complaints about clinical actions by means of an independent professional review by two consultants. The decision as to whether there should be such a review is a discretionary one, taken by the regional medical officer. The HSC can investigate complaints of maladministration in relation to the way the regional medical officer has carried out this function. Similarly, there can also be an investigation of the actions of the health authority in relation to the procedures leading up to or following the decision of the regional medical officer. The HSC can also consider the administrative actions of the indepen-dent consultants who conduct the review (see Longley 1993: 69–70).

This procedure only goes part of the way to addressing the problem caused by this exclusion. The review procedure only deals with the actions of doctors, and does not cover actions taken by nurses, midwives or other professionals, whose actions can, sometimes, involve the exercise of clinical judgement. The Hospital Complaints Procedure Act 1985, which obliges health authorities to establish complaints procedures for hospital patients and to publicize such procedures, came into force in March 1988 (Health Circular 88(37)). Although these procedures are designed to deal with complaints that do not involve the exercise of clinical judgement, some complaints about the actions of these other professionals may be being filtered through administrative procedures under this Act (see Longley 1993: 69, 77).

While it is understandable that there should be some reservations about ombudsman involvement in the judgement of medical professionals, there does seem to be a case for extending jurisdiction to cover this area. There would be no question of the HSC imposing his or her own judgement. The HSC is able to investigate complaints from patients in hospitals that are under the direct control of government departments, which include top-security hospitals at Broadmoor, Rampton, Moss Side and Carstairs, and the Ministry of Defence Hospitals for members of the armed forces. In these cases there is no exclusion preventing an investigation of matters involving clinical judgement. Where a question of clinical judgement arises, the HSC takes medical advice on the clinical aspects of the case. This could be done in other cases.

It is important to note that it is for the HSC, not the clinician, to decide whether the matter complained of comes within this area, but what is or is not a matter of clinical judgement is sometimes difficult to discern. There was a case, mentioned in the *HSC Annual Report* 1985–6, where a psychiatric patient committed suicide and the complaint by a relative was that he was inadequately supervised. This was deemed a matter of clinical judgement. The inquest jury concluded that the supervision was inadequate, but the HSC could not even comment on the inquest verdict.

Another problem was highlighted in the *HSC Annual Report* 1990–1 (see HC 44, 1992: paras 37–9), in relation to a decision not to resuscitate a patient. The complainant complained when he discovered that his elderly mother would not be receiving cardiopulmonary resuscitation in the event of a heart attack. The complaint involved three issues: why the decision not to resuscitate had been taken; why he (the son) had not been consulted or informed; what the authority's policy was on resuscitation. He was dissatisfied with the answers he received and complained to the ombudsman. The HSC could not question the decision not to resuscitate, as this was a clinical judgement made by the doctors responsible for the patient. However, the investigation revealed confusion about the policy of the hospital and whether relatives were normally involved in such decisions. As a result of this case, the authority drew up guidelines on resuscitation (see *HSC Annual Report* 1990–1: 12). This case was the subject of Select Committee investigation, and while there was a satisfactory outcome in relation to this authority, there is no way of knowing whether other authorities and hospitals will do the same.

This particular case illustrates the ability of the HSC to investigate related matters, even though part of the complaint is about clinical judgement. The HSC in post at the time of writing has admitted that he takes his jurisdiction as far as he 'legitimately can to establish whether there are related factors' (*HSC Annual Report* 1991–2: 2). He will therefore investigate procedures or communications which may have impaired the quality of the clinical treatment. These would include, for example, inadequate planning and preparation for a surgical procedure and lack of advice about what to do when a catheter becomes blocked. He does not, however, want matters relating to clinical judgement to be within jurisdiction (HC 650, 1993: 23).

Service committees (para. 19(2)). This exclusion prevents investigation into actions taken by a service committee of the family health services authority (FHSA) in the exercise of its functions, powers and duties under the National Health Service (Service Committees and Tribunal) Amendment Regulations 1990. This means that the HSC cannot investigate complaints about the formal procedure by which these service committees consider allegations that community practitioners (that is, general medical practi-. tioners, dentists, opticians, pharmacists) have breached the terms of their contracts with the FHSA by their behaviour towards a patient (see Longley 1993: 73–4). However, the HSC can investigate the operation of the informal conciliation procedure that FHSAs operate to resolve complaints. There can also be investigations into other aspects of the work of the FHSAs, such as the closure of surgeries and the removal of patients from a doctor's list.

Recently the Select Committee has expressed concern about the voluntary informal complaints procedure operated by the FHSAs. One concern was that this procedure was being used in a more formal manner than was intended, and there was also concern about a proposal to make the procedure obligatory. If it were brought within the formal arrangements, the whole procedure would be removed from the HSC's jurisdiction. Assurances have been received that this will not happen (HC 433, 1989: para. 6). More recently, concern has been expressed about the confusion in the distinction between the formal procedure, which is outside the HSC's jurisdiction, and the informal procedure, which is not. It has been recommended that the distinction between the formal and informal procedures should be made clear, as should the criteria to be applied in judging which procedure is most appropriate for any given complaint (HC 441, 1990: paras 29–31).

Service committee formal complaints proceedings are subject to the jurisdiction of the Council on Tribunals, and they may be subject to judicial review. However, the fact that the HSC cannot investigate 'puzzles and annoys' complainants (*HSC Annual Report* 1991–2: 3). The HSC has commented on examples of poor handling of complaints by FHSAs, and he has *prima facie* examples of maladministration in the operation of the formal procedure. He is prevented from investigating this and, as the Select Committee note, as a result complainants may be 'deprived of potential investigation and redress' (HC 44, 1992: para. 14). The HSC at the time of writing would like to be able to investigate actions taken by FSHAs in relation to the use of the service committee formal procedure for investigating complaints (HC 650, 1993: 23).

Personnel matters (para. 19(3)). Action taken in relation to appointments or removals, pay, discipline, superannuation or other personnel matters are excluded. There are similar provisions in relation to the Parliamentary and local government ombudsmen. However, this may be more problematic in relation to the jurisdiction of the HSC, as members of staff of health authorities and hospitals can take a complaint to the HSC on behalf of a patient. This could lead to problems of victimization of the member of staff

concerned. Recently, this has led the HSC to ask a district health au
concerned in such a complaint to ensure that local procedures pro
member of staff against isolation or victimization (*HSC Annual Report*
1991–2: 4).

Commercial transactions (para. 19(4)). Contractual and other commercial
transactions are excluded, other than matters arising from arrangements
between the body subject to investigation and another body for the provision
of services for patients by that other body. This proviso covers such matters
as relations with private nursing homes taking National Health Service
patients, and therefore a complaint about the way such a patient was dealt
with in such a home could be investigated.

The National Health Service and Community Care Act 1990 allows for
health authorities to arrange for the delivery of services through National
Health Service contracts. This has caused concern in relation to complaints
and the HSC's jurisdiction for such 'contractual' matters. Futhermore, where
a service is provided by a non-National Health Service institution, the patient
might be denied access to proper complaints procedures. The HSC has taken
up these matters with the Department of Health, and has been assured that,
although some of the details are still to be worked out, users of the National
Health Service, wherever they obtain their care, will continue to have access
to the ombudsman if they are dissatisfied (*HSC Annual Report* 1991–2: 4).

A recent case appears to have expanded the scope of the exclusion in
relation to commercial and contractual matters. The HSC has received and
investigated complaints from family practitioners themselves about the
FHSAs with which they have agreed to provide general medical services.
However, in *Roy* v. *Kensington and Chelsea and Westminster Family
Practitioner Committee* (1990) 1 Med LR 328, the Court of Appeal concluded that the relationship was a contractual one, and the HSC has therefore taken this to mean that such cases are outside jurisdiction. The
Department of Health does not agree with this view, but the House of Lords,
although throwing some doubt on the Court of Appeal interpretation, has
not overruled it (see *Roy* v. *Kensington and Chelsea and Westminster Family
Practitioner Committee* [1992] 1 AC 624). The HSC has therefore decided
that, as the relationship is a contractual one, such complaints are outside
jurisdiction.

Section 84 inquiries (para. 19(5)). Action that has been, or is, the subject of
a Section 84 inquiry cannot be investigated. These inquiries were governed
by Section 70 of the National Health Service Act 1946, and are now covered
by Section 84 of the 1977 Act. The provision allows the Department of
Health to set up an inquiry into any aspect of the National Health Service
that the Secretary of State deems advisable. These are rare and would only
occur where there were serious concerns or allegations giving rise to

widespread public concern. However, the decision to hold such an inquiry, and the inquiry itself, might be the subject of a complaint to the ombudsman against the actions of the Department of Health.

DISCRETIONARY POWERS

Under the 1977 Act all matters in connection with the initiation, continuance or discontinuance of an investigation are for the discretion of the commissioner, and questions of whether a complaint is duly made are for the commissioner (Section 113). The HSC cannot investigate any administrative action where the complainant has a right of appeal to an administrative tribunal or a court of law (Section 116), but this section is subject to the proviso that in these cases the HSC has a discretionary power to investigate if, in the circumstances, it is not reasonable to expect the complainant to resort to these remedies. Similar powers are available to the Parliamentary and local government ombudsmen.

If it is clear that a complainant believes that negligence is involved, and is seeking compensation, the HSC will not usually investigate the matter, as it is more appropriate for the courts to determine. However, the ombudsman will use his discretion to investigate such cases if, despite the reference to such things as neglect, there is in fact no intention to pursue the matter through the courts. Concern has been expressed that in these types of cases the HSC was obtaining an undertaking from the complainant that he or she would not sue, which was seen as undesirable and maybe unenforceable (Justice 1988). Even though it was recognized that this practice did allow an investigation where this might otherwise have been refused, Justice (1988: 96) felt that the practice was undesirable in principle, and such an undertaking should only be sought in special circumstances. Indeed, the Department of Health has expressly stated that such undertakings are bad practice and unenforceable in relation to independent professional reviews. The position now appears to be that the HSC, rather than seeking an undertaking, asks for an assurance that it is not the intention of the complainant to take legal proceedings. Although this is not enforceable, it helps the HSC to proceed with a complaint, particularly where the complaint letter seems to indicate that litigation is either likely to be viable or really intended.

MALADMINISTRATION AND INJUSTICE

The HSC has a wider frame of reference than the Parliamentary ombudsman, and can investigate 'an alleged failure in a service provided by a relevant body' or 'an alleged failure of a relevant body to provide a service which it was a function of the body to provide' where the complainant has suffered injustice or hardship as a result of this failure or as a result of maladministration (Section 115). The HSC can thus investigate not only complaints about maladministration in connection with action taken by or on behalf of a National Health Service authority, but also complaints about failure of service. The Parliamentary ombudsman, on the other hand, is confined to examining complaints involving maladministration.

The concept of maladministration has already been discussed in relation to the Parliamentary ombudsman, and the issues connected with it are not significantly different in relation to the HSC. Where there may be difficulty is in relation to 'failure' of service, particularly where this may overlap with questions of clinical judgement. Even if it is not problematic from the point of view of clinical judgement, the main problem may be one of adequate resources. This is a difficult area, as funding of the National Health Service has generated much controversy in recent years. The level of funding is relevant in discussion of alleged service failure but to what extent should resource issues be taken into account? A previous ombudsman, Sir Cecil Clothier, has said that delays are not necessarily maladministration if they result from financial constraints and the need to assess priorities between competing demands for additional posts (HC 419, 1982: 15). Delay in itself is not, therefore, a sufficient cause for criticism. It must reasonably be attributed to maladministration and not to resource problems beyond the control of the department.

However, where the resource problems are within the control of the authority, and decisions have been taken with maladministration, the complaint will be upheld. In one case involving a neglect of duty, the problems of the physical environment were compounded by the inadequate staffing levels on the ward. Nursing numbers were not only below establishment, but were not at the right levels of seniority. Although it was claimed that this was owing to recruiting and financial problems, the HSC concluded that the staff shortages were within the control of the management, particularly as they related to planned leave of absence. It was a management responsibility to plan for eventualities such as study leave, annual leave, maternity leave and staff sickness. There was a marked discrepancy between the general shortage of staff at the hospital and the particularly acute shortage on this ward, which could not be accounted for by reference to recruitment and financial problems (see HC 44, 1992: para. 18).

Section 120 of the 1977 Act prevents a commissioner questioning the 'merits of a decision taken without maladministration by a relevant body in the exercise of a discretion vested in that body'. This limitation on the power to question the merits of discretionary decisions is the same as that imposed on the Parliamentary and local government ombudsmen. Maladministration covers such matters as not following proper procedures or agreed policies, failing to have proper procedures, giving wrong information or inadequate explanations of care, or not dealing promptly or thoroughly with the original complaint.

REMEDIES

The HSC cannot in general offer any financial remedy, and in only a very small number of the cases which are investigated does the possibility of a financial remedy arise. The HSC believes that compensation and damages are matters for the courts, although occasionally he will reimburse for financial loss, and invite or recommend a health authority to make an *ex-gratia* payment. In 1990–1 there were nine cases where a financial remedy was given. The sums involved were modest and included: the cost of a lost nightdress; compensation for lost jewellery; *ex gratia* payment for the cost of travelling to and from hospital for treatment; *ex gratia* payment for distress caused to a woman by the handling of her request for assistance with nursing home fees for her father (*HSC Annual Report* 1990–1: 14). There were only three cases in 1991–2 where the health authority concerned was recommended to provide a financial remedy. These involved: reimbursement for lost clothing; reimbursement of private chiropody charges; *ex gratia* payment in respect of costs of transport to hospital (*HSC Annual Report* 1991–2: 21). The recent annual report indicates that in four cases *ex gratia* payments were made. The largest amount paid was £210, to cover the cost of a private ambulance, when there was a failure to arrange inter-hospital ambulance transport for a patient (*HSC Annual Report* 1992–3: 27).

Financial remedies are rare, and usually involve a small amount of money. However, payment of these sums has not been without problems. A few years ago, on Treasury advice, the Department of Health revised its instructions to health authorities so that all cases involving a compensation recommendation by the ombudsman had to be referred to the department. The reason for this change was that it was felt unreasonable to expect health authorities to make informed judgements about whether a case would create an awkward precedent. Although this involved only a few cases, the result would be to delay an authority's response beyond the two-week deadline expected by the ombudsman. Despite this, it was felt that a balance ought to be struck between delaying the final settlement and setting a precedent which could have ramifications for the entire public service.

The Select Committee thought that to insist on all payments being subject to scrutiny by the Department of Health was excessively bureaucratic, and recommended that the department press for the restoration of the discretion for health authorities where the HSC recommended small sums of money to be paid in compensation (HC 433, 1989: para. 7). It was decided that this discretion should be restored to health authorities, and this was done with effect from 1 April 1990, when the limit of discretion was raised to £5,000. The discretion does not apply in cases where compensation is recommended when there is no cash loss, but these kinds of cases are relatively few (HC 441, 1990: para. 52).

Few remedies involve financial compensation, and only sometimes is a remedy of direct benefit to the complainant. Indeed, the HSC is not just concerned with remedying individual grievances, but places great importance on the contribution made by his office 'to the quality of service which the National Health Service provides' (HC 44, 1992: para. 52). Although the remedying of individual grievances is important, he sees it as equally important to change the system to ensure that a higher standard of service is provided than was provided in the past. In this connection, it is therefore worrying when several investigations involving one authority highlight similar problems.

The remedy proposed by the ombudsman will almost certainly seek to prevent a repetition of similar maladministration in the future. The types of procedural remedies obtained by the ombudsman are indicated in the annual reports. In a recent report, these are categorized into four broad areas (*HSC Annual Report* 1991–2: 22–31). In the first category, the remedies are in relation to administrative practices or procedures associated with medical activity, and these include: reviewing prescribing procedures with the aim of avoiding errors; reminding medical staff of the importance of involving anxious relatives in decisions about how to proceed when operations do not go according to plan; and reviewing arrangements for referring patients between specialties.

The second category is concerned with remedies for administrative practices or procedures associated with action in the ward. These include: a review of discharge procedures; review of procedures to ensure that supervision of patients is maintained during ward handover; clarification of nursing policy on lifting patients; and ensuring that all nursing staff are aware of drug administration procedures. The third category is concerned with administrative practices or procedures associated with action in other hospital departments, and includes remedies to ensure that staff know where available information is located. Also in this category are: a recommendation that the operation of laundry arrangements be reviewed to prevent loss of personal clothing; action to prevent notice of outpatient appointments from being sent to patients who have died; and clearly understood procedures to be laid down so that theatre staff know in good time of the need to obtain any special equipment before an operation.

The final category concerns practices and procedures associated with record keeping, correspondence and complaints. A number of the remedies here suggest that complaints procedures be reviewed, that guidance on complaint handling be reviewed and that staff be informed of their role in relation to the complaints procedure and the implementation of the written complaints procedure. A number of remedies suggest that staff need to be reminded of the relevant procedures for handling complaints and the need to deal with complaints in accordance with the procedures. Many remedies involve the need for staff to be reminded of the importance of record keeping and of keeping relatives and patients informed. Other remedies in this category include: reminding consultants of their responsibilities under the clinical complaints procedure; promoting better communications with relatives and carers; and improving signposting for the benefit of visitors coming to the hospital at night.

Although there is no power to impose a remedy, the recommendations 'are almost invariably accepted by the health authority concerned' (HC 44, 1992: para. 12). The HSC follows up cases to try to ensure that the recommendations have been put into effect. Once a report is issued the follow-up work involves asking the chief executive to report back, usually within three months, on the actual action taken to implement the recommendation. In most cases a satisfactory reply is received. The matter is pursued until the ombudsman is satisfied that every recommendation has been acted upon. Any persistent failure to implement a recommendation would be drawn to the attention of the Select Committee.

Inadequate staffing levels are often highlighted as a result of complaints, together with inadequate supervision of patients or junior staff. Complaints can also highlight problems that involve a lack of guidance from the Department of Health. One such case related to a patient taking part in clinical trials without her consent or knowledge (see HC 44, 1992: para. 68). The department has now issued new guidance on clinical research, which addresses the issues in the case, and local leaflets on clinical trials are being amended to reflect this guidance.

It is rare for health authorities to persist in a refusal to accept the HSC's findings or proposed solutions. If this does happen, the health authority concerned can be brought to the attention of the Select Committee by the HSC. The Committee can then require the health authority to appear before it to give an explanation and answer questions.

One case where a health authority refused to accept the HSC's findings involved a voluntary body that received 90 per cent of its funding from the authority and was providing services under the National Health Service Act 1977. There was a complaint about the voluntary body, and although the authority had a duty to see that the complaint was properly investigated it did not investigate the detail of the complaint. The Select Committee felt that a body providing public funds to another body has a responsibility with regard to any complaints made against that body. However, the authority's view was that responsibility was confined to ensuring that that body was competent and well-run, and properly investigated any complaints made to them. The Select Committee would like this situation clarified (HC 368, 1991: paras 61–3).

PROCEDURE AND POWERS

Section 111 of the 1977 Act provides that complaints can be made by any individual or body of persons, whether incorporated or not, excluding certain public bodies. This is identical to the provisions for the Parliamentary and local government ombudsmen. In the normal course of events, complaints are received from patients or would-be patients. However, complaints can be received from consumer groups. Community health councils cannot make complaints about services directly to the ombudsman, but they can assist or write on a complainant's behalf.

Many patients wish to be accompanied by a relative or friend in the initial stages of making a complaint. The Department of Health has said that a patient complaining can be accompanied by whomsoever he or she wishes to a meeting with consultants, and that this includes the secretary of the local community health council. One complaint to the ombudsman involved a situation where a consultant refused to allow a representative of the community health council to be present at a meeting, although he would allow a relative or friend. Only if the initial meeting failed to satisfy the complainant was the consultant prepared to have such a representative present at a further meeting. The HSC said that the representative could be present as the 'patient's friend' (HC 44, 1992: paras 48 and 49).

The complaint has to be made by the person aggrieved unless the complainant has died or is for any reason unable to act for him or herself (Section 111(2)). In these cases, the complaint may be made by the personal representative, by a member of the family or by some body or individual suitable to act as a representative. 'Suitable' is not defined in the Act, but the ombudsman takes a generous view of this, and few problems have been caused by this requirement. A complainant acting through an agent (for example, a doctor, MP or councillor) is treated as making the complaint him or herself.

As with the PCA, there is a requirement that the complainant must be aggrieved. Despite this, Section 117 provides that any authority complained about may itself refer a complaint to the ombudsman for investigation. This is provided that the complaint is properly made to the authority and is referred to the ombudsman within twelve months from its reception. The time limit under the 1977 Act used to be three months, but this was extended by Section 7 of the Parliamentary and Health Service Commissioners Act

1987, as it was considered that the original time limit caused problems in practice.

Regional and district health authorities can use this procedure where it is obvious that the complainant will not be satisfied unless there is an independent investigation. This procedure may also be used where, for example, a serious complaint is made against senior members of the authority, making it desirable for there to be a completely independent inquiry. This procedure is only used rarely and requires a resolution of the members of the relevant authority. As with the Parliamentary and local government ombudsmen, there is no provision for the HSC to investigate on his or her own initiative, and the HSC at the time of writing does not wish to extend jurisdiction into this area (HC 650, 1993: 35).

The ombudsman will not investigate a complaint unless it has been brought to the notice of the body complained against, and that body has had a reasonable opportunity to investigate and reply to it (Section 112 of the 1977 Act). Failure to put the complaint to the relevant authority is the most common reason why complaints are referred back or not considered to be within jurisdiction (*HSC Annual Report* 1988–9: para. 2.12).

An exception to this provision is where the complaint is made by a member of staff of the hospital or health authority complained about on behalf of a person unable to complain for him or herself. In this case, before accepting the complaint the ombudsman has to be satisfied that there is no one more appropriate to take up the complaint. This exception is important in relation to 'whistleblowers', who express concerns about the safety, health or well-being of patients. Concern about whistleblowers has led to the publication by Derek Fatchett MP of a Private Member's Bill, the National Health Service (Freedom of Speech) Bill, to ensure that staff are able to exercise freedom of speech on issues of patient and client care, and that they are not penalized for speaking out in good faith. The HSC is also concerned about such issues, and this has led him in one case to ask the relevant authority to ensure that local procedures protected a member of staff making a complaint against isolation or victimization (*HSC Annual Report* 1991–2: 4).

There is no residence requirement for complaints to the Health Service Ombudsman, but there is a time bar. The complaint must be made in writing within a year from the date when the complainant first had notice of the matters alleged in the complaint. The ombudsman does not investigate complaints outside this time limit unless she or he decides that it is reasonable to do so (Section 114). The ombudsman may deem it reasonable to waive the time requirement where the delay is caused by the illness of the complainant, or because other remedies have been pursued without success. One difficulty with investigating complaints relating to events in the distant past is the problems caused by the frequent movements of junior staff and the difficulty of tracing locum staff.

Part I of Schedule 13 of the 1977 Act requires that the relevant body or person complained about should be given an opportunity to comment on the allegations made in the complaint. Apart from that, and the fact that the investigation has to be conducted in private, the HSC, like the Parliamentary ombudsman, has discretion on how to conduct the investigation. If the ombudsman decides not to investigate a complaint, any statement of reasons for this has to be sent to the complainant and the body against which the complaint was made (Section 119(2)).

The majority of rejections are usually referrals back to complainants because further information or action by them is needed before there can be a decision by the HSC on whether to conduct an investigation. Many such rejected cases have not gone through the authority's complaints procedure. In some cases the ombudsman will suggest other avenues open to complainants when there is no jurisdiction for the ombudsman to intervene. There have even been some cases of apparent maladministration that lay outside jurisdiction, where the ombudsman was able to take steps informally to see that matters were attended to (HC 44, 1992: para. 5). The Select Committee has welcomed this flexible approach, which is in line with the role of the ombudsman as a check on maladministration in the National Health Service.

When a complaint has been received and accepted, investigators usually go to the authority concerned, examine the files and interview the relevant staff. Most of the HSC's investigations staff are on secondment from the health service or civil service, as it is thought that they have the specialized knowledge which will make it easier for them to detect failings. Investigators invariably interview the complainant, often in his or her home. This is similar to the method of investigation used by the Parliamentary ombudsman, and involves a thorough, high-level review. One of the problems with such a thorough approach is that it can lead to delay, and this has prompted the Medical Protection Society to send a letter to the Select Committee complaining about the delay in investigating complaints and the disruption to health care caused by interviewing those involved in cases (HC 441, 1990: para. 6).

The Medical Protection Society, a defence organization which represents doctors and dentists throughout the world, has a membership of 46,000 in the United Kingdom. The HSC's response to the complaint about delay was that he can accept complaints up to a year from the event and has discretion after then to accept them. This in itself means that cases may be investigated some time after the event giving rise to the complaint. The ombudsman procedure is used as a last resort, so this also involves a delay, as complainants turn to him only when other methods have failed. In defence of the thorough approach, the ombudsman feels that, as there is no appeal from his decision, it is incumbent upon him to ensure that his reports are

thoroughly researched. Although these arguments indicate that the procedure can be lengthy, the ombudsman himself is anxious to reduce the time
taken to reach decisions, and has offered to enter into a dialogue with the
Medical Protection Society about this.

There is no doubt that the time taken to complete investigations is a
source of concern (see HC 441, 1990: para. 5), although more recently
improvements have been noted. Thus the ombudsman's aim of responding
definitively to an original letter of complaint within three weeks was
achieved in three out of four cases in 1990–1. The average time for com-
pleting cases in 1990–1 was fifty-eight weeks, excluding the initial time when
cases were referred back to the complainant, and more than half of the cases
were ready for issue in under twelve months. In addition, the average length
of reports was reduced from thirty-three to nineteen pages. There had also
been a reduction in the average number of separate items of complaint in
each case. The present ombudsman is concerned that matters be dealt with
as speedily as possible, and his three-year management plan for the office
has target times for responses (see HC 44, 1992: paras 7–9). There were
further improvements in 1991–2, the average time taken to complete an
investigation dropping from 58 to 45.1 weeks per case, an improvement of
22.2 per cent. The initial screening process has been reduced from 21 to 18
days, and the average length of report has now fallen to 16.6 pages (*HSC
Annual Report* 1991–2: 2). These achievements are to the credit of the
HSC and his staff, particularly when set against the increasing numbers
of complaints.

Part I of Schedule 13 of the 1977 Act gives power to the ombudsman to
pay towards any expenses incurred in connection with an investigation, and
also powers to ensure that a full investigation can be conducted. These
powers are identical to those of the Parliamentary ombudsman, and include
the power to require the production of documents by the health authority
and to compel witnesses to attend and give evidence. Obstructions of the
HSC in the performance of these functions will be treated as if they were a
contempt of court.

The report made at the end of an investigation is sent to the complainant
and the body against whom the complaint was made. In addition, a copy
is sent to anyone who was the subject of allegations in the complaint and
to the authority having overseeing capacity over the body complained
against (Section 119(1)). For example, a report about a district authority
goes to the regional authority, and one about a regional authority, National
Health Service Trust hospital or special health authority goes to the Secretary
of State.

This particular provision has been called into question in relation to
complaints against National Health Service Trust hospitals. These hospitals
are subject to the HSC's jurisdiction, but they are directly accountable to the

Secretary of State. Some trusts have expressed the view that district health authorities should therefore have no interest in the handling of trust complaints. The deputy commissioner has, however, taken the view that the monitoring of complaints is a feature of quality assurance and contract negotiation, and therefore an essential concern for district authorities. It is a matter of concern, therefore, that investigation reports will not be sent to district authorities when the complaint is against a trust hospital.

Section 5 of the Parliamentary and Health Service Commissioners Act 1987 authorizes the ombudsman to send copies of the report to MPs who have been associated with the complaint. Before this provision the ombudsman had not done so, on the grounds that the report might not be privileged if disclosed to MPs in this way.

CASES INVESTIGATED

In the first year of operation, the HSC received 361 complaints, and this figure rose steadily to 712 in 1978–9. There was then a drop in the following year to 562, followed by a yearly increase, which reached another peak of 926 in 1985–6. The figures for the number of complaints received over the past five years are:

Year	Number
1992–3	1,227
1991–2	1,176
1990–1	990
1989–90	794
1988–9	753

The number of complaints received in 1992–3 was the highest since the office came into being. Although there has been a marked increase in the number of complaints received in recent years, a striking feature of these figures is that overall the number of complaints is small, when set against some 7.5 million admissions to hospitals and 50 million outpatients treated per year.

Only a minority of these complaints result in a final report, and despite the increase in the number of complaints the number of results reports has remained remarkably steady, fluctuating between 101 and 154 each year, apart from 1989–90 when only 89 results reports were issued. Over the past ten years, each case report has contained an average of between three and four grievances. Throughout this time, the grievances upheld have fluctuated between 43 and 61 per cent of the grievances investigated, the highest percentage of justified grievances being in 1987–8. Overall, for the past ten years, 54 per cent of grievances have been held to be justified. It is thought that the high number of justified grievances is partly because the ombudsman is becoming more expert in detecting those cases which are not viable, and partly because advisory bodies like community health councils are better aware of how the ombudsman operates (HC 433, 1989).

On average, over the past ten years the majority of grievances have concerned nurses (38 per cent) and doctors (22 per cent). Complaints about administration have accounted for 18 per cent of grievances, and those relating to a failure in service constitute 6 per cent of all grievances. An average of 16 per cent of grievances are about the way a complaint was handled. Figures from a recent annual report indicate a rise in the number of nursing complaints (45 per cent) and a slight fall in the number of complaints about doctors (20 per cent). The proportion of complaints about administrative matters (8 per cent) was a considerable reduction from the previous year, and 8 per cent of grievances concerned a failure in service. The proportion of investigated grievances about the handling of complaints fell from 22 per cent in 1990–1 to 19 per cent in 1991–2, and 73 per cent of these were found to have some justification. This high proportion of justified grievances in relation to complaint handling is worrying, and the ombudsman has indicated that it is an area of service that health authorities might improve (*HSC Annual Report* 1991–2: 39).

Some of the main types of cases investigated include complaints about the standard of maternity services. These include complaints about the monitoring of progress during labour and inadequate contingency plans to deal with an abnormally high workload, resulting in a delay of some six hours after the birth of her baby before a woman was operated upon for the removal of a retained placenta. Failure to keep a proper check on a patient's progress is a common cause of complaint, as is the provision of long-term care for the chronically ill, where the expectations of relatives and carers of what the National Health Service should provide are not being realized.

Failure in communication among staff, or between staff and patients or relatives, is a recurring theme. The Select Committee has seen fit to comment on this, recognizing that the 'problems that arise through a breakdown in communications are manifold' (HC 368, 1991: para. 28). The ombudsman too has remarked that lack of communication and poor communication are 'at the root of so much of what I have to investigate' (HC 44, 1992: para. 24). Problems in relation to records are a reflection of poor communications. One case demonstrated that 'deficiencies in communications and records are intimately connected with failures in the delivery of care to patients' (para. 24). In one case, there was a loss of records, which hampered the HSC's investigation and was regarded as careless if not suspicious.

The ombudsman also deals with complaints about the handling of clinical matters. Although clinical judgement cannot be investigated, the ombudsman can investigate the administration of independent professional reviews, which were set up some ten years ago to deal with clinical complaints. Many of these cases involve delay. The ombudsman will also investigate cases where it appears that staff have not followed the correct procedures, even though part of the complaint relates to clinical judgement. These kinds of situations include: cases where the correct procedures are not followed when preparing patients for operations; failure to follow good practice guidelines and consult relatives in relation to consent for an operation on a severely disabled adult; and failure to inform a general practitioner of the hospital's policy in relation to treatment for a blocked catheter.

Ambulance services have occasionally been the subject of complaints. In a recent annual report the ombudsman expressed concern that a number of these cases referred to emergency cases where there was unreasonable delay, resulting in a great deal of suffering for patients and their carers (*HSC Annual Report* 1991–2: 12). In one particular case procedures had been changed as a result of investigations, which led the Select Committee to 'welcome the Authority's swift and thorough response to the weaknesses highlighted by the Commissioner's investigation' (HC 44, 1992: para. 33).

The ombudsman has also investigated allegations of maladministration by family health services authorities in their informal handling of complaints against general practitioners. In one such case the ombudsman was critical of the fact that a woman was never informed of the outcome of her complaint.

The ombudsman has been critical of the number of complaints about the way an authority has handled a complaint, particularly as there should be detailed guidance available to all staff who handle complaints (*HSC Annual Report* 1991–2: 14). In one case the HSC referred to a 'catalogue of ineptitude and lack of personal accountability' in the handling of a complaint. This was caused by a lack of proper monitoring, confusion about responsibility for the progress of complaints and the lack of suitable experience by the staff involved in handling the complaint. In another case, the district health authority took some seventeen months to respond to an MP who was acting on behalf of a complainant. In another case, involving property mislaid in hospital, a solicitor received no reply from the hospital after three months. When an investigation into the loss was begun, this was not documented in detail, and a letter sent over five months later to the solicitor said that there was no record of the loss and that the authority could take no further action. Another case involved an appeal in relation to property stolen from a patient while in hospital. Although the hospital indicated that the appeal would be considered by an officer other than the one who had dealt with the original claim, it was in fact dealt with by the same person, a practice which the ombudsman regarded as dishonest (*HSC Annual Report* 1991–2: 14–16).

ACCESS

Unlike the PCA, there is no requirement for complaints to be filtered through an elected member, and complainants complain directly to the HSC. However, complainants must have made their complaint to the health authority concerned, and given the authority an opportunity to investigate it, before the ombudsman can investigate. In this sense, the HSC deals with complaints that have remained unresolved through the internal processes, and this acts as a kind of filter on the complaints that come to the HSC. The exception to this rule is where a complaint is made by a member of staff of a hospital or health authority, acting on behalf of a patient who is unable to complain him or herself. In these cases there is no requirement that the complaint must first be made to the health authority.

Under the terms of Health Circular 88(37), which sets out directions under Section 1 of the Hospital Complaints Procedure Act 1985, formal complaints about hospital services which do not involve the exercise of clinical judgement should be referred to the relevant district health authority. Each health authority must designate a senior officer to deal with complaints. Complaints that are not resolved through these procedures may be referred to the Health Service Commissioner.

The Select Committee has highlighted the importance of effective handling of complaints by health authorities, not in order to replace the work of the HSC but to enable as many grievances as possible to be remedied promptly before cases reach him (HC 44, 1992: para. 70). This is not a new concern by the Select Committee, and as long ago as 1977, in a report on hospital complaints, the committee stated that 'there should be a simple, straightforward system for handling complaints in every hospital with emphasis on listening carefully to the patient's or relative's concern and dealing with it promptly' (HC 45, 1978: para. 41).

Guidance issued by the Department of Health in 1988 on the operation of the Hospital Complaints Procedure Act 1985 does not seem to have had the desired effect of improving the effective handling of complaints at local level. In 1990–1, grievances about the local handling of complaints increased to 22.6 per cent of the total investigated compared to 16.5 per cent in the previous year, and 74.4 per cent of the grievances were found to have some justification, compared to 69.9 per cent in the previous year (*HSC Annual Report* 1990–1: 25). This former proportion was reduced to 16 per cent in the following year, but 73.5 per cent were found to have some justification (*HSC Annual Report* 1991–2: 38). Under the Patient's Charter, health authorities and National Health Service hospitals will have to publish details of the number of complaints received and the length of time taken to deal with them.

PUBLICITY

One of the problems with the HSC is that few people know of the existence of the office. The 1977 Act requires little in terms of publicity. Individual results reports have to be sent to the parties concerned, but these do not have to be made public. The Act requires that the ombudsman makes annual reports to the Secretary of State, who must lay them before Parliament, and there is also a power for the ombudsman to make special reports where injustice has not been, or will not be, remedied, or otherwise as is thought fit (Section 119(3)). In addition to annual reports, the HSC publishes twice-yearly volumes of anonymized complaints, which are submitted to appropriate ministers, together with their epitomes in an anonymized form. However, the ombudsman's reports receive little media coverage, which is partly because they are anonymous. There is more likely to be media interest when there is Select Committee interest in the case. Parliamentary debates on the work of the HSC would be useful in raising the profile of the office.

In a recent annual report the present HSC speculated that 'perhaps too few patients know that my Office exists' (*HSC Annual Report* 1990–1: 1). The Select Committee considers that this is almost certainly the case, and has welcomed the efforts made by the ombudsman to publicize his work and make the office more approachable. The general leaflet relating to the office has been revised in order to make it easier to follow, and to help those making complaints through the procedures. This new leaflet was issued in January 1991 and widely distributed. The HSC has also used various opportunities to explain his work on the radio, in the press and in professional journals. In order to make the office more approachable, the length of reports has been reduced and the language used in them has been simplified.

The Department of Health is also trying to increase awareness of the HSC, and in this context the department has written to the chairs of health authorities about the role of the ombudsman. The department now sends case summaries direct to community health councils (HC 44, 1992: para. 11). More publicity at the point of contact would be useful, so publicity for the HSC should be in hospital wards and outpatients departments. Information about the HSC is now often given on 'how to complain' literature in hospitals.

More publicity would result in more complaints. Indeed, the 19 per cent increase in the numbers of complaints in 1991–2 is seen as resulting from a growing public awareness of how to complain and to whom (*HSC Annual Report* 1991–2: 1). This increase has implications for the work of the office, but the Select Committee believes that this is a welcome sign of the growing awareness of the ombudsman's services (HC 44, 1992: para. 3). More publicity would also raise expectations, and care must be taken that these expectations are not a cause of frustration. The ombudsman is the last resort for complainants, so any publicity should alert complainants to this fact and also involve publicizing the agencies of first resort.

The work of the ombudsman is now being publicized through patient's charters. These have followed on from the Citizen's Charter, the implications of which were discussed by the Select Committee in relation to the PCA. Some aspects of the Citizen's Charter are also relevant for the HSC, as patient's charters all contain references to the role of the HSC and should contribute to a greater awareness of it. The Select Committee particularly liked the Welsh patient's charter, which referred to the fact that the HSC was free and completely independent (HC 44, 1992: paras 50 and 51). In addition, the charter standards, both locally and nationally, should give a clear benchmark to inform patients whether or not they have a right to complain. For example, there is a charter standard that patients will be given a specific appointment time in outpatient clinics and will be seen within thirty minutes of that time (see HC 44, 1992: para. 66).

The patient's charter suggests that complainants should go to the HSC if they remain dissatisfied after complaining to the body responsible. This illustrates that one of the best ways of raising awareness of the HSC is through the internal complaints procedure. The HSC has, therefore, written to the chairs of all health authorities reminding them that local procedures should tell complainants that they have a right to complain to the HSC if they are not satisfied with the local investigation. Although references to the HSC in hospital literature are increasing they are not widespread, and the Select Committee has recommended that the Department of Health should direct all health authorities to include a reference to the HSC in leaflets on hospital complaints procedures (HC 44, 1992: paras 50 and 51).

It is not only among the public that more awareness of the HSC is needed. There is also a lack of awareness of the work of the HSC among health service professionals. Although individual health authorities implement the recommendations of the HSC, these recommendations have wider applicability, as do the lessons to be learnt from an investigation. Many failures keep occurring, and the HSC has lamented that the lessons from investigations are not being learnt as widely as they should be, which causes him concern in his capacity as an external auditor of the quality of service delivered to patients.

The HSC has suggested that his published cases should act as 'a quality audit of the National Health Service, prompting periodic review of local procedures and the transfer of improvements in systems from other areas' (HC 44, 1992: 55). Suggestions for dissemination of information include: distribution of summaries of cases to all health authorities; use of reports in training and seminars; and articles in specialist magazines. Both the HSC and his deputy give talks to National Health Service staff, to try to address this, and they also speak at conferences attended by health service professionals. The Department of Health should encourage health authorities to distribute epitomes widely among their staff, although this does not necessarily mean that the reports will be read. The Select Committee has recommended that when the department distributes these epitomes it should ask the health authorities to report back on the steps taken to disseminate them and to enhance awareness of the HSC's work more generally, which may resolve this problem. The department should also consider collating and distributing a guide to best practice in this field (see HC 44, 1992: para. 55). The ombudsman himself does not feel that it is appropriate for him to publish a good practice guide, but is ready to provide illustrations of where failures can occur (*HSC Annual Report* 1991–2: 3).

CONCLUSIONS

Before a complainant can use the HSC procedure, the complaint has to go to the health authority concerned, and the expectation is that a substantial number of complaints will be satisfactorily resolved by the authority's internal procedure. Thus the HSC scheme has to be assessed in terms of its ability to deal with complainants who have already failed to achieve satisfaction through the initial, internal procedures of the National Health Service, rather than as a first order complaints handling procedure (Giddings and Pearson 1991: 2–3). It should, therefore, be assessed within the context of the total complaints system within the National Health Service. It has to be said, however, that complaints procedures in health authorities are not yet fully developed (Longley 1993: 87).

Sir Anthony Barrowclough, a previous HSC, was convinced of the value of an independent and impartial mechanism for consumers of the National Health Service when the service has fallen short of what they expect. However, the problem with the HSC is that not all complaints can be investigated, and this has led to 'the fragmented pattern of procedures for complaints about National Health Service matters and . . . some areas where there is no provision for outside investigation of complaints' (HC 441, 1990: para. 57). The exclusions from jurisdiction are therefore a serious drawback to the work of the ombudsman.

A further problem is the lack of awareness of the office, and although there has been an increase in the numbers of complaints in recent years, the numbers are still small when set against the numbers of patients receiving treatment by the health service.

The linkage with the Parliamentary ombudsman is a primary feature of the HSC scheme (Giddings and Pearson 1991: 11). Not only do both the HSC and PCA report to the Select Committee, but the two roles are at present, and have always been, occupied by the same person. In May 1991, during a Parliamentary debate on the ombudsman, Sir Anthony Buck mentioned that perhaps the HSC and Parliamentary ombudsman should be two separate persons. This will probably come about because of the increased workload, as more people now complain to both ombudsmen. It will be interesting to compare how the two offices develop if this happens.

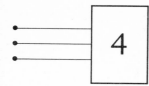

THE LOCAL GOVERNMENT OMBUDSMEN

INTRODUCTION

The exclusion of local authorities from the Parliamentary Commissioner's jurisdiction was widely criticized at the time that office was established, and it was not long before Justice, which had played a major part in preparing the ground for the Parliamentary ombudsman, turned its attention to the question of a local ombudsman. In its report *The Citizen and His Council: Ombudsmen for Local Government?*, published in 1969, it recommended the appointment of one chief commissioner and five or six commissioners for local administration. They would work from a central office, rather than being regionally based, in order to facilitate liaison between them and the Parliamentary Commissioner, and they would investigate complaints of maladministration by local authorities.

In 1970, the White Paper *Reform of Local Government in England* was published, which contained proposals for the establishment of a system of local ombudsmen. This proposed the setting up of ten or more local ombudsmen, based in different parts of the country, who would examine complaints of maladministration by local authorities. By analogy with the Parliamentary Commissioner, and contrary to the recommendations of Justice, complaints would have to be channelled through local councillors, rather than be received directly from members of the public. These proposals fell with the Labour government, but the Conservative government took up the plan for a system of local ombudsmen. Their proposals included nine local commissioners for England, and one for Wales. The commissioners would report to representative bodies of local authorities and water authorities, and they would be financed by local authorities. The Bill incorporating these provisions received the Royal Assent in February 1974, just before a general election.

THE SCHEME

The Commission for Local Administration was set up by Part III of the Local Government Act 1974, which provides for a body of commissioners known as the Commission for Local Administration in England, and a body of two or more commissioners known as the Commission for Local Administration in Wales. The Parliamentary Commissioner is a member of both commissions. Arrangements for Scotland and Northern Ireland were set up by the Local Government (Scotland) Act 1975 and the Commissioner for Complaints (Northern Ireland) Act 1969, respectively. This chapter will concentrate on the work of the English Commission.

The English commissioners are appointed by the Queen on the recommendation of the Secretary of State for the Environment after consultation with the appropriate representative bodies. The Act did not specify the number of commissioners to be appointed, but it did say that the commissioners shall divide England into areas, and that one or more commissioners shall be responsible for each area. England was thus divided into three areas, on a population basis, and a local commissioner was appointed for each area.

Dr D.C.M. Yardley is the Chairman of the Commission, and the local commissioner dealing with complaints from Greater London, Kent, Surrey, East and West Sussex. He is based in London. Mr F.G. Laws, formerly Vice-Chairman of the Commission, moved his office from London to Coventry. His successor, Mr E. Osmotherly, handles complaints from the South West, the West, the West Midlands, Cheshire, Staffordshire, Leicestershire, Cambridgeshire, Warwickshire, Northamptonshire, Bedfordshire, Hertfordshire, Buckinghamshire, Berkshire, Oxfordshire, Essex, Norfolk, Suffolk, Hampshire and the Isle of Wight. The third local commissioner and Vice-Chair of the Commission is Mrs P.A. Thomas. Based in York, she deals with complaints from Derbyshire, Nottinghamshire, Lincolnshire and the North.

The Parliamentary Commissioner for Administration, Mr W.K. Reid, is an ex-officio member of the Commission, but he takes no part in the investigations carried out by the local commissioners. His membership is useful, as it enables the Parliamentary ombudsman and Local government ombudsmen to share experiences, to compare notes on how problems are tackled and to consider matters of mutual interest. The three ombudsmen from Wales,

Scotland and Northern Ireland normally attend the quarterly meetings of the Commission for Local Administration in England, by invitation, thus ensuring that all seven of the UK statutory public sector ombudsmen meet on a regular basis. Mr M. Mills, ombudsman for Ireland, also attends.

The Commission's main objective, which is set out in each annual report, is the investigation of complaints of injustice arising from maladministration with a view to securing, where appropriate, both satisfactory redress for the complainant and better administration. The authorities whose administrative actions are subject to investigation by the local government ombudsmen were listed in Section 25 as follows: any local authority; any joint board of local authorities; any police authority, other than the Secretary of State; any water authority. Water privatization has meant that jurisdiction over water authorities has ceased, but recent legislation has brought in other bodies. The relevant authorities subject to the local government ombudsmen's jurisdiction are: district, borough, city or county councils (not town or parish councils); the Commission for New Towns or new town development corporations (housing matters only); urban development corporations (town and country planning matters only); housing action trusts; police authorities; fire authorities; any joint board of local authorities, including the National Park boards; the National Rivers Authority (flood defence and land drainage matters only); the Broads Authority.

The ombudsmen are therefore in a position to consider complaints against all types of local authorities, dealing with significant areas of local administration. In practice, the vast majority of investigations involve local councils, and the Commission has now decided that in future the informal title of local commissioners will be local government ombudsmen (LGO), in order to make explicit that the responsibilities of the local commissioners are confined almost entirely to local government (*CLA Annual Report* 1990–1: 4).

The Commission has developed a number of supporting objectives, which take into account the duties imposed by statute. These are:

- to encourage authorities to develop and publicize their own procedures for the fair local settlement of complaints and to settle as many as possible;
- to encourage the local settlement of complaints made to the local government ombudsmen;
- to make the local government ombudsman system known as widely as possible and to advise people how to make their complaints;
- to secure remedies quickly for those whose complaints are justified;
- to issue guidance on good administrative practice to local government and to relevant bodies;
- to guide those with complaints outside the jurisdiction of the local government ombudsmen;
- to support the work of other ombudsmen.

The Commission was set up primarily as a method of handling individual grievances involving local authorities. But the work is not confined to individual issues, and it is important to note that as well as 'satisfactory redress' the aim is to achieve 'better administration'. The great bulk of the work, however, does centre on individual grievance handling, and this is certainly how the LGO see their role, being of the view that the primary concern is to secure a remedy for an individual's grievance. Only after this is the concern to help individual authorities to administer better and to encourage better practices generally.

JURISDICTION

The local government ombudsmen are empowered to investigate complaints of injustice arising from maladministration occurring after 1 April 1974, but are not allowed to question the merits of decisions taken without maladministration by authorities in the exercise of their discretion (Local Government Act 1974, Section 34(3)). The distinction between the merits of a decision and how that decision was reached is not always clear, and in R v. *Local Commissioner for Administration: ex parte Bradford Metropolitan City Council* [1979] QBD 278, [1979] 2 All ER 881, the court said that Section 34(3) does not preclude the investigation of acts on the ground that they are decisions taken by a local authority on the merits of a case, as taking a decision is an action taken in the exercise of an administrative function. In this case, a mother was complaining to the local government ombudsmen about the local authority's actions in respect of her children, who had been taken into care by the authority and placed with different foster parents. The court said that the actions of the authority could be investigated, and that the LGO had jurisdiction to deal with any maladministration which may have occurred in the council's handling of the children.

However, in the case of R v. *Local Commissioner for Administration: ex parte Eastleigh Borough Council* [1989] 1 All ER 1033, it was held that the local government ombudsman had exceeded his jurisdiction because the ombudsman's report had gone beyond a criticism of the council's failure to follow its own policy, and had questioned the merits of the policy decision in relation to the inspection of drains. It had been decided in the lower court that, despite the fact that jurisdiction had been exceeded, there could be no relief to the council, as this would in effect provide a right of appeal against the ombudsman's findings. The Court of Appeal, recognizing that the case raised 'issues of some importance concerning the relationship between courts and the local ombudsman' (per Lord Donaldson, p. 152), decided that the LGO's report was subject to judicial review in cases where jurisdiction had been exceeded.

Apart from the limitation imposed by Section 34, there are some *administrative* actions that are outside the jurisdictional limits of the ombudsman. For example, the LGO is prevented from investigating 'general matters' by Section 26(7) of the Act. This provides that a commissioner shall not investigate a complaint about the action of an authority which in his opinion 'affects all or most of the inhabitants of the area of the authority concerned'. This prevents an investigation of a complaint concerning improper expenditure or other wrongful action on financial matters. The LGO decides whether a complaint comes within this exclusion, and provided that the question has been considered fairly, the decision is not open to question.

Although Section 26 empowers the LGO to investigate complaints in connection with administrative action taken by the authorities mentioned above, it also precludes investigation in respect of matters described in Schedule 5 of the Act. Expressly excluded by this Schedule are matters concerned with the internal affairs of schools, personnel matters, action taken in connection with the commencement and investigation of legal proceedings, and commercial and contractual matters. These Schedule 5 exclusions will now be discussed in turn.

The commencement or conduct of court proceedings (para. 1). This exclusion prevents the investigation of the commencement of civil or criminal proceedings, and the conduct of proceedings when they have been started.

Local authorities have many powers where there is a criminal sanction attached, and thus a decision on whether to commence proceedings in such cases, or a failure to do so, could be construed as coming within this exclusion. For example, it could be argued that a complaint about the failure of a council to take action following an unauthorized cutting of trees is covered by this exclusion, as it is a criminal offence to lop trees in a conservation area unless the local authority is notified of the intention to do so.

Such an interpretation would lead to the exclusion of many, if not most, enforcement complaints. It appears that the local government ombudsman can investigate the local authority's actions when they are deciding whether to serve an enforcement notice, but cannot investigate the decision not to take action in the magistrate's court. It seems that this exclusion is not rigidly adhered to, because if it were then very little would be within jurisdiction, because criminal proceedings are often possible, even if remotely.

The government view concerning this exclusion is that *administrative* actions taken before court proceedings are within jurisdiction already, and there is no case for extending jurisdiction beyond this (Government Response to Widdicombe 1988: 29). There has been a recent case where the LGO investigated a complaint that a local authority had failed to exercise its powers to deal with the unlawful eviction and harassment of a tenant in privately rented accommodation (CLA case report 89/A/1581).

Commercial and contractual matters (para. 3). This exclusion prevents the local government ombudsman from investigating actions taken by a local authority relating to contractual matters or commercial transactions, and its inclusion in Schedule 5 appears to be because there is a similar exclusion in the 1967 Act for the Parliamentary Commissioner. The schedule specifically excludes from jurisdiction transactions relating to the operation of harbour undertakings, the provision of entertainment, the provision and operation of industrial establishments, and the provision and operation of markets. However, the exclusion does *not* cover transactions relating to the acquisition or disposal of land, so matters dealing with tenancies, leaseholds and mortgages are within jurisdiction. For example, a complaint about the way a council decided to give or withhold a licence to assign a shop lease is within jurisdiction. The exclusion does not cover transactions in the discharge of functions under any public general Act, other than the functions required for the procurement of goods and services in connection with those functions. Tendering matters are contractual, and therefore outside jurisdiction.

This is a wide exclusion and the local government ombudsmen and their staff want to see an end to it. In the Commission's fourth review, they urged the government to include within jurisdiction the administration of market operations and the provision of moorings (*CLA Annual Report* 1991–2: 58). The Secretary of State has agreed to consult on these issues.

There are cases concerning commercial enterprises where the exclusion has not been relevant, for example concerning delays about registration of private residential homes for the elderly (CLA case reports 88/C/1377, 0776). Nor has the exclusion prevented the investigation of two cases (CLA case reports 87/C/205, 706) which involved the use of an unreasonable and misleading method to select firms of undertakers with a view to advertising their services, and which resulted in certain firms being given an unfair advantage. There have also been investigations into complaints about unreasonable delay in determining applications for hackney carriage licences, resulting in loss of earnings (CLA case reports 86/C/0647, 1100, 1101).

Justice (1980: 13) has argued that commercial and contractual matters should be within jurisdiction. Widdicombe (1986: 22) was not convinced that commercial and contractual matters with members of the public were 'different in kind from cases involving other local authority dealings with the public', and a review of the exclusion was called for. The government, however, has argued that ombudsmen are concerned with 'the interaction between the executive arm of Government and the general public', and that actions taken by public bodies in buying and selling services are 'fundamentally different' (Government Response to Widdicombe 1988: 29). Their view is that there is no case for providing protection through the local government ombudsmen, as there are legal safeguards and remedies.

However, some areas are to be kept under review. These are where the commercial aspect is almost a secondary function, such as the allocation of market stalls and the use of non-commercial considerations in tendering procedures.

The LGO makes the point that some traders may be highly dependent on business from their local authority and that if that business is unfairly denied them, their livelihood may be threatened. The Commission is seeking alteration of the law 'to allow investigation of complaints about the way proposed contracts are allocated or withheld' (*CLA Annual Report* 1988–9: 54). In relation to this, the Local Government Act 1988 places a duty on public authorities to give reasons for certain decisions relating to contracts. The Act imposes a duty on local authorities to exclude from contracts any consideration of matters which are non-commercial, and there is therefore a duty not to discriminate against a contractor by the introduction of political or irrelevant considerations (Section 17). Where this section applies, the authority must give written reasons for: a decision to exclude a contractor from an approved list; a decision not to invite tenders, or not to accept them; or a decision to terminate a contract (Section 20).

These provisions were tested in the case of *R* v. *London Borough of Enfield: ex parte I.F. Unwin (Roydon) Ltd* (1989) 46 Build LR 1, where a contractor was suspended from Enfield's list of approved contractors, the only reasons being that there were 'inquiries into the conduct' of the borough's staff. Unwin, the contractor, started proceedings for judicial review, seeking orders of mandamus requiring reasons for the decision to suspend it from the lists of contractors, and an order of *certiorari* to quash the decision, arguing that there was a statutory duty to give reasons by virtue of the Local Government Act 1988. Enfield did not deny that it had failed to comply with the duty imposed by Section 20, but said that there were 'substantial and serious allegations of offences or irregularities in the relationship' between Enfield and Unwin, and that while the allegations were being investigated by the police it was not possible to provide further details to him.

The court accepted the dilemma of local authorities in cases such as these, and decided that the standard of fairness which a contractor was entitled to expect depended on all the circumstances. In this case, the fact that an investigation was under way did not deprive Unwin of the right to be told of the accusations and to be given a chance to answer before a decision was made. In the circumstances, Enfield was not justified in failing to give reasons for its decisions, and because of the prior relationship with the council Unwin was entitled to a legitimate expectation of fair treatment.

The courts are thus becoming involved in these areas, whereas the local government ombudsmen are excluded. Cases such as this strengthen the need for an extension of jurisdiction to complaints about the method of awarding or withholding contracts.

Personnel matters (para. 4). This exclusion relates to action taken in respect of appointments, removals, pay, discipline, superannuation and other personnel matters. The reasoning behind the exclusion is that employment law should be uniform in the public and private sectors, and that personnel matters are really to do with collective bargaining and industrial relations. However, the exclusion also relates to potential and ex-employees, who would not be protected by collective bargaining procedures. The exclusion does produce anomalies. For example, a delay in paying housing benefit can be investigated, but a delay in paying a local authority pension to an ex-employee or his or her family cannot. Furthermore, maladministration could be found if an application for council property was lost, but not if an application for a job with a local authority was lost.

Other countries do have such jurisdiction. For example, in Australia, the Commonwealth Ombudsman investigates complaints relating to recruitment, compensation and retirement benefits (see Commonwealth Ombudsman 1983–4). Since 1976 the French Mediateur has been empowered to receive complaints from former or retired public servants (see Clark 1984: 171).

Although Widdicombe (1986) saw that the primary function of the local government ombudsmen was 'to provide support for the consumers of local government services rather than those who are employed to provide them', concern was expressed about potential staff, and a code of practice was recommended governing officer appointment procedures, breach of which would constitute *prima facie* maladministration, which would allow an applicant to complain to the LGO (p. 221). It appears that the main concern here is with the so-called 'political appointees' (p. 156), and while the government do not want to extend the ombudsman's jurisdiction in this area, they are taking steps to prevent 'politically biased or prejudiced selection and appointment procedures' (Government Response to Widdicombe 1988: 30).

In general, however, the government considers that personnel matters are essentially concerned with relations between employer and employee, and not with the relations between a public authority and the public, and that therefore they should not be subject to LGO scrutiny (Government Response to Widdicombe 1988: 30). The LGO considers that personnel complaints, except from those currently employed by the authority against which they wish to complain, should be within jurisdiction. However, it has been decided not to pursue the matter at the present time (see *CLA Annual Report* 1988–9: 54).

Internal school and college matters (para. 5). This exclusion refers to any action taken by a local education authority in the exercise of its functions in relation to instruction within schools. It is extremely wide, and excludes most of the matters relating to the internal affairs of any school or other educational establishment run by a local authority. It excludes matters to do with conduct, curriculum, discipline, internal organization and management. It does produce anomalies. For example, there can be an investigation into the treatment of a child in a local authority home, but not in a local authority school.

Education departments themselves do come within the local government ombudsmen's jurisdiction but they generate comparatively few complaints. In recent years education complaints have made up between 4 and 6 per cent of all the LGO's complaints for each year, with about the same percentage of formal investigations. The exception to this was 1984–5, when there was an increase, making education complaints 7 per cent of all complaints and 9 per cent of all formal investigations. This increase was due to complaints about school admission appeal committees, and they simply reflected the teething problems of a relatively new system. There were fewer complaints of this sort in the following year, and the pattern followed previous years. Only a handful of complaints are rejected by the LGO each year because of this exclusion, but there is no way of knowing how many more complaints there would be if the exclusion were abandoned.

As well as producing anomalies, the exclusion has also resulted in some strained interpretations. For example, in one case, a child was suspended from school in circumstances where the local government Ombudsman said that he felt the child should have received help from an education psychologist. In the report there was criticism of the local authority and the school, although the LGO has no jurisdiction to examine the conduct of the school (CLA case report 82/J/5509). In another case (CLA case report 87/A/961) there was a finding of maladministration because of the poor treatment of a pupil after an incident at a school. The LGO has also investigated a complaint about the council's delay in informing the parents of a child who had had an accident in the school playground of the results of the council's investigation into the matter (CLA case report 90/B/306).

This exclusion has been the subject of some debate, and Justice (1980: para. 43) has criticized the exclusion and recommended that internal school matters should be brought within jurisdiction. It was recognized, however, that implementation of this may not be feasible in the immediate future, for reasons of cost and limited resources.

In the 1980–1 Annual Report the local government ombudsmen endorsed the view that internal school matters should be within their jurisdiction in the same way that complaints about matters internal to any other local authority establishment are within jurisdiction. They suggested that if it is right that a complaint can be made about the internal running of a children's home, then 'in principle it must be right also that a complaint can be made about the internal running of a children's school' (*CLA Annual Report* 1980–1: 43). This has been the consistently held view of the LGO, a view restated in the 1988–9 Annual Report, where they said that they saw no logical reason why any action of a local authority in the exercise of their administrative functions should be outside the local government ombudsmen's jurisdiction (*CLA Annual Report* 1988–9: 54).

However, research has found that education department officers are in general against such an extension (see Lewis *et al.* 1986: 27). There is a belief that the existing system is adequate because of the numerous regulations covering internal school matters, and because of the important role played by school governors in grievance resolution. It is suggested that the LGO would be overwhelmed with complaints, and that therefore an extension of jurisdiction is not practical. Even so, these officers recognized that the extension of jurisdiction would give an opportunity for a problem to be dealt with by an independent body, and some education department officers could foresee no problem with investigations into internal *administrative* matters, for example failure to teach the correct set book or failure to enter a pupil for an examination.

There is no question but that the local government ombudsmen would only be able to investigate 'administrative' actions as in other local authority areas. Indeed, if the LGO could investigate internal school matters it seems unlikely that there would be a huge increase in workload, as the limits of maladministration would themselves exclude many complaints. Under the Education Reform Act 1988, Section 23, local authorities are to set up complaints procedures to receive complaints in respect of the curriculum and related matters. It appears that the local government ombudsmen have not received any complaints in relation to this.

There has been some emphasis on the role of school governors in dealing with complaints. During its existence, the Representative Body felt that it would be both impracticable and undesirable for an outside body such as the Commission to be able to investigate complaints about the internal arrangements of schools, and that there were other ways of examining complaints, for example by school governors (*CLA Annual Report* 1980–1: 61). However, school governors can be ill-equipped to perform this role. They do not, and cannot, act as ombudsmen, and cannot guarantee impartiality. They can be less objective than education departments, and in many cases are unwilling to override the wishes of headteachers. The Education Reform Act 1988 has altered the functions and roles of governing bodies, and only time will tell whether the changes will prove effective in improving the handling of complaints, although it does seem that governors will be less able to act as ombudsmen independent of the schools, particularly as schools themselves are now being given increased autonomy from local authorities.

The Education Reform Act 1988 has reduced the impact of the

ombudsman in relation to some schools. The Education Act 1980 established appeal committees to hear appeals about the admission of children to schools and about the exclusion of children from school. These appeal committees are within the jurisdiction of the local government ombudsmen. However, appeal committees for grant-maintained schools, which were created by the Education Reform Act, are not within jurisdiction. In addition, appeal committees established by the governors of voluntary-aided and special agreement schools are not within jurisdiction. The Commission is concerned about this and is recommending amendments so that all statutory appeal committees would be within jurisdiction (*CLA Annual Report* 1990–1: 7). The government has recently announced that it proposes to bring in legislation to allow the LGO to investigate all such complaints (*Guardian* 20 October 1992).

Despite the general criticisms of the exclusion in relation to internal school matters, the government has come out strongly against the extension of jurisdiction. Some matters, such as allocations, catchment areas, grants and school buses, are within jurisdiction, but the government does not consider it desirable to extend jurisdiction to 'the control and instruction of children within school', as this is a 'professional rather than an administrative function' (Government Response to Widdicombe 1988: 29). This is a serious drawback to the LGO's role of resolving individual complaints but the Commission has decided not to pursue the matter any further at the present time (see *CLA Annual Report* 1988–9: 54).

One other restriction imposed by the 1974 Act prevented the LGO investigating actions taken in connection with the investigation or prevention of crime (Schedule 5(2)). The government, in its response to the Widdicombe Report, accepted that this exclusion was not necessary, except in relation to police authorities (Government Response to Widdicombe 1988: 29), and it has been amended by Order in Council (The Local Government Administration (Matters Subject to Investigation) Order 1988, SI 1988 No. 242). The amendment enables the local government ombudsmen to investigate actions taken in connection with the investigation or prevention of crime, except in the case of police authorities.

There appears to be little justification for the majority of the Schedule 5 exclusions. However, during its existence the Representative Body, supported by the Department of the Environment, was hostile to any extension of jurisdiction in these areas. Widdicombe (1986) recommended extension in some areas, and the LGO themselves agree that their role is unnecessarily and sometimes illogically restricted. It could be argued that the LGO should be able to investigate all local authority matters, except where there are positive justifications for not doing so, as in defence matters. In its reviews, the Commission has consistently recommended to the Secretary of State for the Environment the need to remove many of the exclusions, with only limited success. In the recent review, the Commission repeated its view that complaints about injustice alleged to have arisen from maladministration relating to all administrative action of a local authority should be within jurisdiction and open to investigation, unless an alternative remedy is available (*CLA Annual Report* 1991–2: 58). The present exclusions can be a source of dissatisfaction and confusion for complainants and they undermine confidence in the ombudsman system itself.

DISCRETIONARY POWERS

Under the 1974 Act, the LGO cannot investigate an administrative action where the person aggrieved has a right of appeal, reference or review to a tribunal or minister, or where there is a remedy by proceeding in a court of law (Section 26(6)). This section is subject to the proviso that in these cases the LGO has a discretionary power to investigate reviewable or appealable decisions if it is not considered reasonable for the complainant to resort to these remedies.

In August 1976, certain criteria were approved by the commissioners for the exercise of discretion in these types of case (see CLA 1990: 2.1–03). Favourable consideration would be given to complainants where the complainant was unaware of his or her right, and the authority failed to advise him or her of it; where the complainant was prevented by absence, illness or some other incapacity from resorting to appeal; and where there was no possibility of bringing an out-of-time appeal.

Some cases would be dealt with on their merits outside of these guidelines, but if there is a specific statutory right to appeal, the LGO are unlikely to accept the complaint. If, however, there is a possibility of enforcement by judicial review, the LGO will not normally expect a complainant to risk incurring high costs to achieve a small benefit. If the complaint concerns a failure to comply with contractual obligations that are within the LGO's jurisdiction (for example, housing repairs), then this will normally be accepted for investigation. The LGO will not accept for investigation complaints about property rights and claims for negligence, except where the complaint is about the *way* the claim was handled or there are high costs compared to the benefits to be gained.

Where the ombudsman is not excluded from investigation by any of these provisions, there is still a discretion whether or not to investigate. Section 26 provides that the commissioner *may* investigate, and therefore it is a matter for the ombudsman to decide. It appears that the courts will be very reluctant to interfere with a decision by an LGO not to investigate a complaint. In *R* v. *Commissioner for Local Administration in England: ex parte Newman and another* (1987) Court of Appeal (Unreported), the court said that Section 26 of the Local Government Act 1974 gave the commissioner a discretion whether or not to investigate a complaint. While not precluding the possibility of judicial review in some (extreme) cases, as the 1974 Act specifically states that 'any question whether a complaint is duly made . . . shall be determined by the Local Commissioner' (section 26(10)), in this case the court said that it was not in a position to substitute its own views for that of the commissioner.

Section 26(4) provides a time bar of twelve months. The LGO, or a councillor, will have to have received, in writing, notice of the complaint within twelve months of the date that the complainant first had notice of matters alleged in the complaint. Where the complaint is out of time, the ombudsman has discretion to accept it. Section 26 has been amended by the Local Government Act 1988 to give greater discretion to the ombudsman to accept complaints out of time. Instead of there having to be 'special circumstances' the ombudsman can accept such complaints where it is 'reasonable' to do so (Schedule 3, para. 5).

MALADMINISTRATION

Part III of the Local Government Act 1974 empowers the LGO to investigate a complaint that a member of the public has 'sustained injustice in conse-quence of maladministration' in connection with action taken by a relevant authority (Section 20). As is the case for the Parliamentary ombudsman, maladministration is not defined by statute, although one could probably suggest that certain actions (or inactions) would give rise to such a finding (for example failure to follow procedures, failure to fulfil statutory duties, failure to keep proper records, unreasonable delay). Stacey (1978: 207) observed that it was clear that the commissioners were classifying as maladministration a great many faulty procedures which were detrimental to the complainant.

More recently the LGO appear to be taking a strong stand against poor procedures, and recent reports seem to reveal a trend towards insisting on certain minimum standards. For example, incomplete record keeping has been criticized (CLA case report 88/A/0015), as has poor liaison between departments (CLA case report 88/A/1067), lack of records of an inspection in building work (CLA case report 87/B/1245) and a case where files had gone missing (CLA case report 88/C/1727). In that case the ombudsman criticized the council's handling of the complaint as being 'less than ideal'.

There is growing evidence that the LGO regards the giving of reasons as a basic requirement in administration, breach of which will give rise to maladministration. The ombudsman has declared in one case (CLA case report 88/A/2329) that good administration 'requires that reasons are given for administrative decisions, and a proper note should be made of such decisions'. This was referred to as a 'breach of elementary administrative procedure', which gave the impression that decisions are arbitrarily made. The ombudsman insisted that the council should 'immediately minute and disclose reasons'. This indicates a step in the right direction, and supports Sir Harry Woolf's view that a duty to give reasons helps administrators to come to the correct decision, and encourages better decision making. Indeed, he regards the giving of satisfactory reasons for a decision as 'the hallmark of good administration' (Woolf 1990: 92–3).

Further developments in the area are encouraging, notably the expectation that all local authorities have internal complaints procedures, and that 'a failure to have one or to rely on one which is incomplete or inadequate may lead to a finding of maladministration' (*CLA Annual Report* 1988–9: 6). This is borne out by the case reports. For example, in one case (CLA case report 87/A/453) the ombudsman declared that 'good administration requires that authorities should have effective and clear internal complaints procedures', and that a 'failure to have arrangements whereby legitimate complaints may be dealt with speedily and fairly may well in itself amount to maladministration'. One report (CLA case report 87/A/961) criticized an authority's failure to have a proper complaints procedure to deal with complaints made about the handling of an incident at a child's school. In another case (CLA case report 88/A/0763) the authority was criticized because there was no evidence to suggest that complaints had been properly investigated, and 'little attention was paid to them at all'. One authority that did have a complaints procedure was criticized because it was not adhered to (CLA case report 88/C/1083). These developments are interesting, particularly as there is no statutory requirement for local authorities to have comprehensive complaints procedures.

Particular problems that confront local authorities are in relation to staffing and resources. The LGO recognize these problems but will not allow them to excuse maladministration. For example, in one case (CLA case report 88/A/0709), which concerned delay in finding a place in a new school for a child who had been expelled, the ombudsman knew that the authority had 'severe staffing and resource difficulties', but nevertheless found that the delay constituted maladministration. In some 'right to buy' cases (CLA case reports 88/C/1692, 88/A/833, 88/A/1341, 88/A/1412) the ombudsmen 'sympathise' and 'do not underestimate the difficulties' which councils have to face when their scarce resources are inadequate, or they fail to recruit staff, particularly in legal departments. Nevertheless, it was found that the failure to meet the timescale imposed by statute constituted maladministration.

In a case involving delay in processing an improvement grant (CLA case report 88/A/1054) owing to acute staff shortages and financial difficulties, the ombudsman would not allow this to 'serve as an excuse for a failure to undertake a duty imposed by an Act of Parliament'. It is difficult for the LGO to find otherwise when there is a clear statutory duty and statutory timescale but, equally, if the councils are employing their resources and staff in the best way one wonders whether such findings can solve the problem. It is interesting to contrast this approach with that of a previous Parliamentary ombudsman, who has said that unreasonable delay was not sufficient in itself to constitute maladministration. The delay had also not to be attributable to financial constraints or resource problems beyond the control of the department (see Rawlings 1986a: 141).

Justice (1988: 133–4) has pointed out the hostility to the word 'maladministration', maintaining that it means little to many complainants, and that, unlike the LGO, the PCA is not bound to use the word 'maladministration' in reports. However, there seems to be little support for a change in this area.

INJUSTICE

Section 31 of the Local Government Act 1974 provides that the authority concerned only has to consider a report where there has been a finding of *injustice* caused as a result of maladministration. Thus maladministration without individual injustice will not require any action from the authority concerned, emphasizing once more the LGO's primary role as being concerned with the individual complainant. There may be poor procedures and maladministration revealed during the course of the investigation, but without injustice, statute requires the authority to do nothing. However, the LGO take the view that if poor practices are unearthed in the investigation, the authority should take action to put things right, despite the fact that there has been no injustice caused.

In some cases where there has been a clear case of maladministration the injustice caused is limited in its extent. In one case (CLA case report 87/B/1350) the injustice was the fact that the complainant had had to correspond with the council and pursue the matter over an unnecessarily long period. This approach is reflected in some of the remedies suggested. In a case (CLA case report 88/B/0774) where the injustice was found to be the loss of a business opportunity, this was to be remedied by a payment 'to reflect the time and trouble involved in pursuing the complaint', and in another case (CLA case report 88/B/110) the council was asked to apologize and pay £100 to the complainant for his 'time and trouble'. In other cases, compensation has been asked for in recognition of distress and anxiety (CLA case reports 89/A/2948, 89/A/1581).

It could be argued that the requirement for a finding of injustice should be abolished, as there is no need for the local authority to respond if there is a finding of maladministration but no injustice. However, this does not seem to have caused particular problems, and there are no calls for change at the moment.

REMEDIES

If an LGO reports a finding that injustice has been caused to the complainant in consequence of maladministration, the local authority has, by virtue of Section 31 of the 1974 Act, a duty to consider the report and notify the ombudsman of the action taken, or what action is proposed to be taken. The action taken by local authorities falls into two broad categories. First, there is actual redress for the complainant, by a reconsideration of the decision or compensation. Second, there could be a review of procedures by the authority to try to prevent similar maladministration occurring again.

Local authorities have legal authority to make payments to redress grievances by virtue of Section 1 of the Local Government Act 1978. This amended Section 31 of the 1974 Act, by adding a subsection empowering authorities to make any payment that appears to them to be appropriate in the light of the contents of the LGO's report. Where an authority wishes to settle a case before the LGO has investigated, the Secretary of State has indicated that the local authority may apply for sanction to make the payment pursuant to Section 19(1) of the Local Government Finance Act 1982 (see *CLA Annual Report* 1983–4: Appendix 4, para. 15).

Where the authority does not notify within a reasonable time, or where the ombudsman is not satisfied with the action proposed, or no action is taken by the authority, Section 31 provides that the ombudsman must make a further report. It has to be said that the majority of local authorities do their best to remedy the injustice as identified by the LGO, although sometimes they are slow to respond. Justice observed that 25 per cent of authorities took longer than six months to respond (Justice 1988: 120).

Not all authorities, however, are prepared to accept the ombudsman's decision. The Select Committee on the Parliamentary Commissioner has noted that 6 per cent of the recommendations of the local government ombudsmen have been without effect, and 19 per cent of authorities that have had an adverse report at one time or another have been prepared to ignore the local government ombudsmen's recommendations (HC 448, 1986: para. 8). By 1992 there had been 186 cases in total since the LGO office was set up where a local authority has not provided a satisfactory remedy after a finding of maladministration and injustice, which represents about 6 per cent of all cases of maladministration and injustice (*CLA Annual*

Report 1991–2: 40). There is no parallel in this respect with other ombudsman systems, none of which, except that for Northern Ireland, has a statutory power of enforcement. However, other ombudsman systems often have the power to make reports to their parliament. The PCA can do so, and is assisted in this respect by the Select Committee on the Parliamentary Commissioner for Administration. But the LGO reports to many different local authorities, whose attitudes to critical reports can vary greatly.

One of the present ombudsmen has admitted that he is constantly trying to avoid issuing further reports because this is 'a very weak thing to do' (see Justice 1988: 121). Harlow and Rawlings (1984) note that the Commission has developed an extra-statutory procedure, to avoid issuing further reports. If it seems that the authority will not take appropriate action, a meeting is arranged with leading councillors and officials, and the LGO tries to persuade them that it is right to provide redress (p. 212). Non-compliance is therefore a serious problem, a problem which was also recognized by Justice (1988: 121), which felt that it was bringing the LGO into disrepute. If a report is not accepted, a further report is issued, which in turn can be ignored. This is in contrast to the vast number of complainants who are obliged to accept findings that go against them.

One solution to the problem is a proposal to adopt the Northern Ireland system of enforcement in the county courts. Under the Northern Ireland system, if there is a finding of maladministration and injustice the complainant can apply to the county court, which may award such damages as it thinks just in all the circumstances to compensate for the loss or injury suffered. The amount of compensation can include expenses reasonably incurred and the loss of opportunity of acquiring a benefit. The court can also grant injunctions (Commissioner for Complaints (Northern Ireland) Act 1969). The report of the commissioner is accepted as evidence of the facts stated, unless the contrary is proved, but the court has a discretion as to the remedy to be provided. In the case of the LGO, both the complainant and the local authority have an opportunity to read and agree with or object to the findings of fact before the LGO reaches a conclusion and makes a final recommendation. Therefore, if such a system were adopted in England, both the LGO's judgement and the court's award would be based on facts about which all parties have either agreed or had a chance to dispute.

The Select Committee decided not to recommend court enforcement (HC 448, 1986: para. 3), but recommended that its remit should be extended to allow the possibility of offending authorities being brought before it to explain their position. If there were no improvement, there should be enforcement through the courts. Justice (1988: 126) saw problems with the Select Committee recommendations, as they involved an encroachment on the independence of local government, and their implementation was 'likely to be so hazardous that it should only be adopted if there is no better answer to hand'. Himsworth (1986) notes that the Select Committee has radically changed its view on this. In 1980, it thought that it was inappropriate to seek to call before it such democratically elected bodies to account for their actions. In 1986, it was wishing to extend its remit. Himsworth does not believe that such a proposal will work, because to rely on 'external buttresses' from ministers, courts or select committees may do more to undermine the LGO than to support their authority (p. 550).

Widdicombe (1986: 220) came close to recommending enforcement following the Northern Ireland model, recommending that 'consideration be given to the application of similar rules' for the local ombudsmen in England. However, enforcement through the courts could create its own problems. Enforcement could make local authorities defensive, and many might want procedures to become more judicial. Investigations could become more lengthy and costly, and authorities might object that there was no opportunity to test the facts by cross-examination. It could therefore become counter productive. Justice (1988: 131), on the other hand, takes the view that the fears of delay and formalism are exaggerated, and that the report should be taken as conclusive, except for the nature and extent of the remedy required, which would be decided by the courts.

The government has rightly pointed out that the 'failures', although small in number, undermine the credibility of the local government ombudsman system as a whole, and that steps should be taken to improve this. However, the government originally thought that the 'independent, informal, flexible investigation of individual complaints without powers of compulsion' remained appropriate, because local authorities might be less willing to cooperate, and investigations might become 'increasingly formalised, lengthy, legalistic and costly' (Government Response to Widdicombe 1988: paras 6.20–6.24).

As a result of this, the government decided against court enforcement in 1988; nor did it like the Select Committee (HC 448, 1986) proposal that the Select Committee has a role in calling recalcitrant councils into account, because 'local government . . . do not see themselves as accountable to Parliament – though recognising that they operate within a statutory framework' (Government Response to Widdicombe 1988: para. 6.23). The remedy proposed was 'more local pressure' and some method of ensuring that adverse reports are fully and properly considered by councils, which should give a 'full and public explanation' if they decide not to comply with the recommendation (para. 6.25).

The 1974 Act did not provide for the local authority to consider formally a further report. This could have been an oversight, or it may have been that it was assumed that all local authorities would comply with the LGO's recommendations, and that further reports would be an extremely rare occurrence. Non-compliance would be mainly due to an oversight, and a further report would act as a reminder. This situation was rectified by Schedule 3 of the Local Government Act 1988, which provides that an authority must consider further reports, and notify the LGO of the action it proposes to take.

New measures were also introduced by the Local Government and Housing Act 1989 in relation to initial and further reports. Section 26 amends Section 31 of the 1974 Act, by introducing changes to the procedures which authorities must follow in considering reports of the local government Ombudsmen. When injustice following maladministration is found, the authority has to consider the report and notify the ombudsman, within three months, of the action it has taken or proposes to take to remedy the injustice. This three-month period can be extended by agreement. The authority then has three months (or longer, by agreement with the ombudsman) to confirm that the action has been taken.

If there is no satisfactory response from the authority, a further report must be issued. Section 28 of the 1989 Act amends Section 31 of the 1974 Act, by providing that a decision not to comply with a further report must be taken by the full council. If a member of an authority is named and criticized in a report, or further report, that member will not be permitted to vote on any question in respect of the report. If an authority does not satisfactorily respond to a further report, the ombudsman may require the authority to publish a statement in a local newspaper, specifying the recommended action they have *not* taken, and, if they wish, their reasons for not complying with the ombudsman's recommendations (Section 26). By 31 March 1992, there had been eighteen cases, involving eight different councils, where the LGO required the council to publish a statement (*CLA Annual Report* 1991–2: 5).

All this puts councils under a greater obligation to state publicly why they do not intend to implement a remedy required by the local government ombudsman. This is an attempt to make the fact of non-compliance a matter of public debate, and it may have the effect of making the system more vigorous, while at the same time ensuring that proceedings remain voluntary and informal. If this proves ineffective, alternative methods may have to be considered. The Commission has previously urged that if voluntary compliance continued to be unsuccessful, judicial enforcement of remedies should be introduced. The current position is to see how the new proposals affect the situation, before any further consideration is given to judicial enforcement (*CLA Annual Report* 1988–9: 54). There is a promise held out in the 1991 White Paper on the Citizen's Charter that the LGO's recommendations may be made legally enforceable if difficulties of non-compliance continue. This represents a complete change of attitude by the government in just three years.

PROCEDURE AND POWERS

Section 27 of the Local Government Act 1974 states that complaints can be made by any individual or body of persons, whether incorporated or not, excluding certain public bodies. Complaints can thus be made by companies, amenity societies, housing groups and partnerships, as well as by an individual. Complaints must, in general, be made by the person aggrieved by the maladministration, but a representative can act where the person has died or is for some reason unable to act for him or herself. In these cases the complaints would be made by the personal representative, member of the family or any other suitable representative of the person aggrieved.

This provision prevents complaints by those who have not themselves suffered injustice through maladministration, even though they may allege that others are aggrieved. It does not prevent social workers or other interested parties bringing a complaint on behalf of others. Indeed, in a recent initiative by the LGO, voluntary organizations have been contacted concerning complaints about social services departments, urging them to make complaints on behalf of clients, who may be unable to make, or have difficulty in making, complaints (*CLA Annual Report* 1988–9: 58).

There is no requirement that the complainant be a resident, charge payer or elector in the area of the local authority concerned. The complainant does not even have to be resident in the United Kingdom. The complaint does, however, have to be in writing (Section 26). Although this is not out of line with most ombudsman systems, there are notable exceptions. For example, the Commonwealth Ombudsman of Australia allows oral complaints, which have now become more common than written ones (see Commonwealth Ombudsman 1983–4). This requirement may present an obstacle to some complainants, although there seems to be no pressure for change. A complainant need not specify the actual maladministration, only the action of the local authority alleged to have constituted it (*R v. Local Commissioner for Administration: ex parte Bradford Metropolitan City Council* [1979] QBD 278, [1979] 2 All ER 881). The complaint can be by letter or complaint form.

Before the ombudsman investigates a complaint, he or she must be satisfied that the complaint has been brought to the notice of the authority concerned, and that the authority has had an opportunity to investigate and reply to the complaint (Section 26(5), 1974 Act). There is no statutory requirement for authorities to have authority-wide complaints procedures, although there are statutory requirements for social services departments, and some education department functions. However, the local government ombudsmen do encourage such procedures, placing a much greater emphasis than the PCA on encouraging authorities to improve and publicize their own grievance procedures (see Rawlings 1986a: 92).

As long ago as 1974, Redcliffe-Maud recommended the adoption by local authorities of clearly established, well publicized procedures for the reception and investigation of complaints by members of the public (Redcliffe-Maud 1974). In 1978 the Commission itself, in consultation with the Local Authority Associations, issued a Code of Practice for local authorities in relation to complaints (CLA 1978), and the LGO believe that it is a mark of good administration to have a proper and effective complaints procedure (*CLA Annual Report* 1986-7: 3).

Despite this, research in 1986 found that only 45 per cent of authorities had authority-wide procedures for handling complaints (Lewis *et al.* 1986: 9). However, the situation does seem to be improving, and in a recent annual report the local government ombudsmen were pleased to note an increasing interest by councils in 'developing their own procedures for trying to resolve their residents' complaints in an effective and economical way' (*CLA Annual Report* 1990-1: 27). It has also been noted that more councils have introduced complaints systems (*CLA Annual Report* 1991-2: 5). The 1978 Code has now been replaced by a new document, *Devising a Complaints System* (CLA 1992). This improvement in complaints procedures has resulted in a higher proportion of complaints being settled locally, without the need for an ombudsman report (*CLA Annual Report* 1990-1: 9).

In addition to providing for an opportunity for authorities to comment on the allegations made in the complaint, Sections 28 and 29 of the 1974 Act provide for the procedure in respect of investigations. There are powers to require information and documents to be produced, and to compel the attendance and examination of witnesses. Crown privilege is excluded in relation to enquiries of government departments, and the LGO has all the powers of the High Court to compel the production of documents or the giving of evidence. Any obstructions in this respect may cause the offender to be dealt with as if a contempt of the High Court had been committed (Section 29, 1974 Act). Powers are also given to reimburse complainants and others for expenses.

Section 32 of the 1974 Act protects the LGO from actions for defamation, and information obtained by the LGO is not to be disclosed except for the purposes of writing the report, or in connection with court proceedings for perjury, breach of the Official Secrets Acts or obstruction of the LGO. Section 32(3) of the 1974 Act, as interpreted in the case of *Re: A complaint against Liverpool City Council* [1977] 2 All ER 650, gave an authority the power to withhold documents or information from the LGO, where it was thought in the public interest to do so. As a result of this case, the section was amended by Section 184 of the Local Government and Planning Act 1980, to ensure that the LGO has a right of access to information and documents relevant to the investigation. A local authority or a minister may serve notice on the LGO that to disclose such information or documents would not be in the public interest, in which case the LGO may not publish the information unless the notice is discharged by the Secretary of State.

The investigation must be conducted in private, but other than this, the LGO has discretion on how to conduct the investigation. The Commission has devised its own procedure for dealing with complaints, which is divided into three stages (see CLA 1990: 3.2–01). The first stage involves an initial appraisal of the complaint to see if it is within the LGO's jurisdiction, relates to an authority which can be dealt with by the LGO and is clear as to what the complaint is about. If a complaint is perceived to be within the jurisdiction of the PCA or HSC, it is forwarded to them. Complaints against other bodies are returned to the complainants with such advice as is necessary. If the complaint is unclear, further details are requested from the complainant.

If the complaint is within jurisdiction and there is a *prima facie* case established of maladministration and injustice, the complaint goes into the second stage. Here the local authority will be asked to comment on the allegations. It may be that this shows that the authority has acted reasonably, or that the injustice claimed would not justify the cost of investigation. If so, the complaint may be rejected, and the complainant informed by letter of the reasons for the rejection. Sometimes a complainant is given an opportunity to respond to this letter before a final decision is made.

It is often necessary, at this stage, to make enquiries of the local authority about the circumstances surrounding the complaint, and if so, the chief executive of the authority will be contacted. If a *prima facie* case is established, the LGO may invite the local authority to settle the case, making appropriate suggestions as to a remedy. If, however, the local authority gives answers that satisfy the LGO, the complaint may be rejected. The complainant will be asked to comment on the authority's response, and on the basis of this the LGO will decide whether to reject the complaint or take it to the next stage. If the authority does not give a satisfactory response, and the complaint seems well founded, the complaint will progress to the next stage.

The LGO refers to this stage as the Stage II investigation (see CLA 1990: 3.2–02), and its purpose is to establish all the relevant facts, so that a decision can be made about whether there has been maladministration. In the great majority of cases, an investigator visits the local authority concerned, examines files, and interviews the relevant officers, complainant and anyone else involved in the case. As a result of these enquiries, it may be that no fault is found with the authority. The investigation will therefore be terminated, and reasons given for this to the parties.

In other cases, where maladministration is found, a draft report is prepared and sent to both the authority and the complainant for comment.

The draft report contains only the factual part of the report, not the LGO's conclusions and recommendations, and its circulation to the parties is an attempt to obtain an agreed statement of the facts. The draft report may be amended in the light of the comments received, and the final report is then prepared. A copy of the report is sent to the complainant, the chief executive of the authority and the referring councillor, if there is one. The report usually contains a recommendation as to an appropriate remedy. Copies of reports are usually sent to local newspapers, and members of the public can take copies of the report, subject to a reasonable charge being made by the authority.

The thoroughness of the investigation procedure has been noted in the past (see Stacey 1978: 221), and recent research (Lewis *et al.* 1986: 60) endorses this view. The taking of oral evidence is a particularly impressive feature of the system, and most of the world's ombudsmen appear to regard this feature of the British practice as the best in the world (see Gwyn 1982).

There are few criticisms of the working practices of the LGO. In common with the other ombudsman systems in Britain the procedure is thorough and rarely restricted to an examination of the documents, except in the most straightforward of cases. A report on working practices was received from the management consultants, Coopers and Lybrand, in 1989. It dealt with organization, operational procedures, workload, information systems, office location and information technology. The report found that working practices were sound, and that there was no need for any major change in the approach to the handling of complaints 'if the present quality of service was to be maintained' (*CLA Annual Report* 1989–90: 9).

One concern is the time factor. The average time taken for a complaint not subject to full investigation is 17 weeks. This is an improvement on the previous year, when it was 18.5 weeks, and was the target set in the business plan (*CLA Annual Report* 1991–2: 31). The Commission is looking at ways of streamlining the work, and is aware of the need to improve efficiency without prejudicing the quality of service. One innovation is to experiment with the use of shorter reports (Meriden 1991: 37).

Research has found that local government officers are satisfied with the thoroughness, fairness and impartiality of the LGO's procedures (Lewis *et al.* 1986: 55). The general impression is that local government looks favourably on the LGO, a fact commented upon by the ombudsmen themselves:

> For the most part local authorities respect and value the Local Ombudsman system, realising that they and we both have our part to play in ensuring that the most reasonable standard of local administration is maintained within the limits of human frailty.
>
> (*CLA Annual Report* 1989–90: 18).

There is no appeal against the findings of the LGO, although the reports are subject to judicial review (see *R* v. *Local Commissioner for Administration: ex parte Eastleigh Borough Council* [1988] 3 All ER 151). In one case (*R* v. *Local Commissioner for Administration: ex parte Croydon* [1989] 1 All ER 1033) the High Court granted a declaration that the LGO's finding of maladministration was unjustified.

CASES INVESTIGATED

In every year since its inception, the number of complaints to the Commission has increased. Although there has been a dramatic increase in recent years, it should be noted that, as with the PCA, the number of complaints is negligible when compared with the number of decisions taken daily by administrators. The vast majority of complaints considered are not investigated to the point of issuing a full report, as Table 3 indicates. Some are rejected initially because they are outside jurisdiction, or because there is no *prima facie* case of maladministration. Some are concluded after initial enquiries have been made. In the majority of cases this is because the evidence shows no injustice or maladministration. In other cases there is a local settlement, or again the complaint is found to be outside jurisdiction. The number of complaints proceeding to a final report has decreased from about 8 to under 3 per cent in the past five years.

Although only a small number of complaints result in a final report, many councils settle issues satisfactorily after a complaint to the LGO. For example, in 1991–2, 1,735 (16 per cent) complaints were settled locally (*CLA Annual Report* 1991–2: 32). In many of these cases there may have been a finding of maladministration if the authority had not averted the need for it by admitting some fault, and doing enough to remedy it to the satisfaction of the LGO. It is probably more accurate, therefore, to say that in nearer 20 per cent of cases the complainants' efforts in registering their complaints produced a satisfactory result.

Table 3　Numbers of complaints

Year	Complaints received	Formal reports	Maladministration found
1991–2	12,123	352	321
1990–1	9,169	319	254
1989–90	8,733	317	259
1988–9	5,908	308	242
1987–8	4,128	332	249

Source: CLA Annual Reports

Every year the subject that attracts the most complaints is housing, which accounts for between 39 and 41 per cent of all complaints. These types of complaints often involve: failures and delays in respect of repairs to council houses; failures and delays to house or rehouse those in need of council accommodation; problems in relation to the payment of housing benefit; delays and failures in considering and awarding improvement grants; delays and incompetence in relation to 'right to buy' cases. Not surprisingly, these complaints are mainly against inner city authorities, which have large numbers of council houses.

Planning matters are the next most popular type of complaint, accounting for between 28 and 30 per cent of complaints each year. These complaints tend to dominate those received from the more rural authorities. They are often about: failure to consult neighbours about a proposed development; failure to take proper account of objections made to a proposed development; giving incorrect or unclear advice about the need for planning permission; failure to enforce planning conditions.

Education departments generate about 6 per cent of all complaints, and these typically involve: failure to provide free transport to school; problems concerning the allocations of pupils to schools; delays and incompetence in dealing with educational awards; failure to have proper complaints procedures. A common subject of complaint is in relation to special educational needs, and more reports were issued in this area than in any other (*CLA Annual Report* 1991–2: 7). Complaints about environmental health account for just less than 4 per cent of complaints each year. Typically, these involve complaints about failures to control noise, smells or other nuisances. The third most common subject of complaint by 1992 was regarding the administration of the community charge and business rate (*CLA Annual Report* 1991–2: 51).

There has been an increase in the number of complaints about social service departments in recent years, and they now account for nearly 4 per cent of cases. Although there are still a small proportion of the LGO's workload, this is a significant increase (from 3 per cent) and may be partly owing to the LGO's initiative in writing to voluntary organizations in 1988 reminding them that they could act on a complainant's behalf (see *CLA Annual Report* 1989–90: 11). Another reason may be the requirement under the Children Act 1989 and the Community Care Act 1990 for social services departments to establish complaints procedures that refer to the role of the LGO (*CLA Annual Report* 1991–2: 31). Many of these complaints are about failures or delays in relation to aids and adaptations for the physically handicapped. Some relate to failures to deal properly with children in care, including failures to give proper advice about access to such children. Maladministration has also been found in some of these cases, where there has been a failure to have adequate arrangements for dealing with legitimate complaints.

STAFFING

Unlike the Parliamentary Commissioner, the local government ombudsmen come from a variety of backgrounds (for example, personnel management, the diplomatic service, academic lawyer, councillor, town clerk). They are not all from local government and some have been legally qualified. The Commission employs investigators and other support staff, and the investigators, too, are from a variety of backgrounds. Stacey (1978: 226), writing soon after the establishment of the office, found that the 'morale of the Commissioners and their staff is high and they have already made a considerable impact'. This seems still to be the case, with staff being of high quality (see Lewis *et al.* 1986: 56).

Investigators are grouped into three teams, each working with one ombudsman, and under each ombudsman is a director. The Commission had 147 staff in post at the end of March 1992: 63 in London, 39 in York and 45 in Coventry. Unlike the PCA's staff, the investigators need not be seconded but can occupy permanent positions. This can pose its own problems. A permanent staff needs a career structure, and there does not seem to be an obvious career structure for these generally highly talented individuals within the Commission. Indeed, it would be a rare occurrence in ombudsman circles for an investigator to progress to the position of ombudsman.

The alternative would be to use seconded staff, like the PCA. In Northern Ireland, staff for the ombudsman's office are seconded from the Northern Ireland civil service, and time spent in the ombudsman's office is seen as valuable career development. Indeed, the incentive for seeking such secondments is the hope of promotion on return to the civil service department. It appears that the Commission made a decision when the office was set up to appoint its own staff, rather than have secondments, on the grounds of loyalty and quality. Unlike in Northern Ireland, it seems that time spent in the LGO's office is not necessarily seen as beneficial for a local government officer's career (Meriden 1991: 38).

Investigators are not local government specialists, although many are from local government. If specialist advice is needed for a problem, opinions are sought from the relevant professional bodies. Generally speaking, investigators are trained on the job, although when one of the ombudsmen recently moved the office to Coventry, a special three-month training programme was devised, because twenty new investigators were all recruited at the same time.

ACCESS

Since the Local Government Act 1988 removed the member filter, complainants can now complain directly to the LGO (Schedule 3, para. 5). Section 25(2) of the Local Government Act 1974 had provided for the submission of complaints to the LGO to be made through a local councillor. Despite the fact that the Act did allow the ombudsman to dispense with this requirement where a member had refused to refer a complaint (Section 26(3)), the provision had been extensively criticized (see, for example, Justice 1980) and many local government officers and members themselves felt that the requirement could no longer be justified. In some authorities officers would, after detailed investigation, actually encourage members to submit complaints, especially in the case of tiresome complainants or resistant complaints (see Lewis *et al.* 1986: 23).

The justification for the 'filter' principle (which existed only in Britain and France) appeared to be that the local authority should have an opportunity of investigating the complaint itself. However, as there is a statutory obligation (Local Government Act 1974: Section 26(5)) on the local government ombudsman to ensure that this has been done, the member filter appeared superfluous.

The provision also mirrored the similar provision in relation to the Parliamentary ombudsman, where complaints are filtered through MPs. It lent support to the idea that councillors are the appropriate people to take up complaints on behalf of their constituents, and that the system was designed to strengthen the hand of local councillors in the same way that the PCA helps MPs. In other words, the LGO service was designed to supplement the traditional democratic process, rather than supplant it.

However, the analogy with MPs was never really appropriate. Councillors have a different constitutional position to MPs, having executive authority, and a much clearer relationship with the services for which they are responsible. They may be asked to complain about a decision in which they have played an active role, which would call into question their independence in relation to the council.

There is also evidence that councillors' commitment to complaint handling may be dependent upon political pressures, with complaints being taken up more vigorously by opposition members (see Birkinshaw 1985: 68). Despite the fact that, within local government, it is councillors who are thought of as the check upon bureaucracy, part-time, unpaid councillors cannot be expected to devote more than a small amount of their time to following up the grievances of constituents. In addition to this, many members of the public may regard the member as part of the organization complained against (a not unreasonable assumption, given the extent to which local councillors are bound up in the decision making process) and may be reluctant to seek his or her help in submitting a complaint.

An additional problem with the member filter was that the member's conduct itself may have been the reason for the complaint. Under the Local Government Act 1972, Sections 94–98, if a member has any pecuniary interest, direct or indirect, in any contract, proposed contract or other matter, and is present at a meeting when it is discussed, she or he must disclose that fact and refrain from the discussion and voting. Breach of this duty is a criminal offence. In addition to this, the standing orders of the authority may provide for the exclusion of such members from the meeting, with the proviso that the member may remain if the majority of those present at the meeting so decide. In addition to this statutory obligation, the National Code of Local Government Conduct (Department of the Environment 1990) gives guidance to councillors on their conduct. The code primarily covers non-pecuniary interests, although it does also refer to pecuniary interests. It has statutory status and councillors must declare that they are guided by it. There have been cases where councillors' actions have been called into question and, although they are exceptional, they do illustrate the problem of relying too heavily on councillors as champions of complainants.

Before the law was changed the Commission had devised its own method of dealing with direct complaints. Since 1984 all complaints received directly were referred to the civil leader with a request that they be settled locally, or formally referred by a member (HC 448, 1986: 46). Many local authorities adopted practices to deal with these so that members (sometimes the leader of the council or lord mayor), sponsored them as a matter of routine. In Scotland, the Scottish Local Ombudsman developed a practice of following up directly referred complaints after one month to see if satisfaction had been achieved (see Bratton 1984: 13).

Such practices are now no longer necessary, and in the first year after the new provision became law, the number of complaints rose by 44 per cent (*CLA Annual Report* 1988–9: 4). This increase is partly attributed to the growing public awareness of the Commission's services, but it also illustrates the disincentive imposed by the member filter in discouraging what may have been valid complaints. Indeed, a comparison of the figures for the year ending March 1989 (where 72 per cent of complaints were sent directly to the ombudsman and 28 per cent were referred by members) with those from 1988 (42 per cent sent direct, 58 per cent referred by members) demonstrates that the removal of the member filter has had a significant effect on the method by which people send their complaints to the local government ombudsmen (*CLA Annual Report* 1988–9: 10).

Since 1989 there has been an annual increase in the number of complaints sent directly to the ombudsman. In 1991–2, over 90 per cent of all complaints received were sent direct, the total number of complaints received that year being 12,123 (*CLA Annual Report* 1991–2: 30). These figures support the view, expressed many years ago by Baroness Serota, that the member filter was 'no more than another barrier between the citizen and the Local Ombudsman' and that 'the people most in need of help are often those ill-equipped to overcome such barriers' (*CLA Annual Report* 1982: Foreword).

INITIATING COMPLAINTS

The requirement imposed by Section 27 of the 1974 Act, that complaints must be made by or on behalf of a person aggrieved, precludes the LGO from investigating complaints on their own initiative, where they have not received a complaint. For example, if they see a report in the media of child cruelty, or the abuse of the elderly, where a local authority is involved, in the absence of a complaint they cannot investigate. Even if the 'complainant' is deceased, or too inadequate to complain, no matter how much the LGO may wish to investigate, and even if the local authority requests an investigation, without an aggrieved member of the public bringing the complaint there can be no investigation.

Despite the fact that many ombudsmen worldwide enjoy such a power (for example, New Zealand, Australia, Denmark and Sweden all empower their ombudsmen to investigate on their own initiative), the local authority associations and the Department of the Environment have always strongly opposed such investigations. Some feel that such a power would alter the nature of the system from being a means whereby citizens can seek an independent examination of their complaints, to being a general overseer of administration in local authorities. Against this, it could be argued that in New Zealand and Australia this power has been exercised sparingly, and one could probably expect the same patterns to emerge in Britain if there were such a power. Given resource constraints, it is likely that own-initiative investigations would only be done very rarely.

Where a local authority requests an investigation, it is difficult to see the objection, provided the LGO is willing and has the available resources. Local authorities often see the local government ombudsman as a highly desirable way of resolving complaints which are found to be difficult or resistant. Such a power would allow the ombudsman to conduct *ad hoc* inquiries where the local authority was in agreement, and would go some way towards Sir Guy Powles's call for ombudsmen to be 'general investigating authorities', a role which has become increasingly recognized by governments worldwide (Powles 1979).

The LGO themselves would welcome the power to initiate investigations, arguing that as the service exists to investigate possible injustice caused by maladministration, it should not be hindered by the fact that a complainant is not readily forthcoming, perhaps because he or she is dead. They believe that there are cases, observed in the media, which appear 'more significant and serious than some complaints properly referred to the ombudsmen by individuals' (*CLA Annual Report* 1984–5: Appendix 4, para. 20). It is felt that such a power would be particularly useful in child abuse cases, as it would be cheaper than an inquiry, would have the advantage of being conducted in private and there would be the power to compel the attendance of witnesses and the production of documents. In addition, the LGO is well established and already has a team of able and experienced investigators (*CLA Annual Report* 1991–2: 6).

Widdicombe (1986: 222) recommended that the local government ombudsmen should have power to initiate investigations 'where there was reason to suppose that injustice had occurred', provided that there was 'good ground for concern', and that it was not used to conduct an investigation into the general procedures of an authority rather than an individual case. Justice (1988: 135), too, believes that the LGO should have the power to make general investigations, without a complaint, provided that the local authority consents or the Secretary of State gives approval. This would not be an overlap with the powers given to the Audit Commission by the Local Government Finance Act 1982, which enable investigations by the Audit Commission into local authorities (Sections 26 and 27). The Audit Commission's concern is the protection of the public as chargepayers, whereas the LGO is dealing with the effects of administration upon individuals.

The government view, however, is that such a power would be a departure from the principle of redressing personal injustices on the complaint of aggrieved persons, and as such the local government ombudsmen could 'lose goodwill and co-operation by acting, or appearing to act, as a general purpose watchdog'. They therefore refused to support it (Government Response to Widdicombe 1988: 30).

As has already been mentioned, the Commission has encouraged voluntary organizations to refer complaints to it on behalf of aggrieved persons. Although this initiative is specifically designed to make social services departments more responsible to their clients, it does represent some attempt to alleviate the problems caused by the prohibition on investigation on the ombudsman's own initiative. The number of complaints received in this way has not been great, but the LGO believes that the letter may have had the effect of encouraging voluntary organizations to recommend the service to clients, who have then complained direct (*CLA Annual Report* 1989–90: 12). Indeed, a 15 per cent increase in complaints received about social services recently may have been a result of this initiative (*CLA*

Annual Report 1990–1: 35), although it could have been caused by a greater awareness in general of the LGO.

PUBLICITY

The provisions for publicity for the LGO are more extensive than those for the Parliamentary ombudsman. Section 30 of the 1974 Act provides that where the ombudsman has completed the investigation, or decides not to conduct one, he or she must send a report to the complainant, to the member who referred it, if applicable, and to the authority concerned. The reports are to identify the authority concerned, but are otherwise to be anonymous. The one exception to the requirement for anonymity is where a member is found to be in breach of the National Code of Conduct (Department of the Environment 1990). In that case, the LGO is obliged to name that member unless she or he considers that it would be unjust to do so. The reports are open to public inspection for a period of three weeks, and this fact must be drawn to the attention of the public by advertisements in local newspapers or other appropriate means. Thus, every investigation report is usually published, although the ombudsman does have power to direct non-publication (Section 30(7), 1974 Act).

The local press and sometimes the national press publicize the reports, although they tend to concentrate on the ones that are critical of the council concerned. There is, not surprisingly, more media interest when the local authority refuses to do what the LGO wants than when there is a successful outcome.

Although these obligations in relation to publicity are more rigorous than for the Parliamentary ombudsman, it is of concern to the Commission that large numbers of the public are not aware of the local ombudsman (*CLA Annual Report* 1988–9: 8). One study found that only 38 per cent of those who took part in a survey had heard of the LGO, and this figure dropped to 2 per cent when the reference was to the Commissioner for Local Administration. When asked to whom they would complain if a local authority did not resolve a complaint satisfactorily, only 13 per cent mentioned the LGO, compared to 40 per cent who would take the matter up with their MP (Lewis *et al.* 1986: 22). In an attempt to alleviate the problem a revised booklet has now been published, which is available from local authorities, Citizens Advice Bureaux, consumer advice centres and other voluntary organizations.

The ombudsmen travel widely and work hard in the interests of publicity, taking up opportunities for radio and television interviews when possible. They have organized a series of seminars for local authorities on complaints systems, which emphasized the importance of making reference to the LGO in the complaints procedure. In addition, MPs are sent a copy of the annual report (Meriden 1991: 33).

Each year there is an increase in the number of complaints (in the year ending 31 March 1992 there were 12,123 complaints compared with 9,169 complaints in the previous year), which is probably a result of improved publicity, and it is interesting to note that the local government ombudsman has always had a much higher number of complaints than the Parliamentary ombudsman, usually four or five times as many. Certainly the LGO have done more to publicize the service than the PCA has (see Birkinshaw 1985: 146).

THE REPRESENTATIVE BODY

The Representative Body ceased to exist on 1 April 1990 (Section 25, Local Government and Housing Act 1989). Section 24 of the 1974 Act had provided for the establishment of such a body, to consist of bodies appearing to the Secretary of State to represent local authorities. The Representative Body consisted of members from the local authority associations (the Association of County Councils, the Association of District Councils and the Association of Metropolitan Authorities) and one representative from the water authorities.

Its function had been to receive and comment upon the annual reports of the Commission and the individual reports made by each ombudsman. It could also comment on any recommendations made or conclusions reached by the Commission in carrying out its statutory duty of reporting on the operation of the Act. It also reviewed the budget, which the Commission prepared, of its estimated expenditure. In relation to this function, it could make comments to the Commission, and ultimately to the Secretary of State, if the Commission insisted on proceeding with a budget estimate which the Representative Body regarded as excessive. Since 1989, funding has been provided directly from the Revenue Support Grant (Local Government Planning and Land Act 1980, Section 56(9)).

Throughout its existence the Representative Body had been criticized in most quarters, particularly for its opposition to reforms of the LGO, especially in relation to the extension of jurisdiction. Lewis (1979: 597) argued that an 'immediate reconstruction of its role and function is perhaps the most urgent reform required in the local ombudsman field'. Birkinshaw (1985: 143) noted the unsupportive nature of the Representative Body, and it certainly never occupied a similar role in relation to the LGO as that taken by the Select Committee in relation to the PCA.

The Representative Body was never particularly supportive of the LGO, and so did not help a great deal in relation to individual reports that found maladministration and injustice which were not accepted by the local authority. In 1982, the LGO invited the Representative Body to help in relation to non-compliance by authorities. The Representative Body is recorded as having felt that 'outside pressure on the matter was unnecessary and ill-founded'. It did agree to recommend to individual local authority associations that they should write to their members urging positive and speedy compliance, but the associations declined to do so (see *CLA Annual Report* 1982–3: 7, 12; *CLA Annual Report* 1983–4: 38).

Justice (1980: 28) recommended its abolition, and thought that it would assist the LGO if a new body were established which was more impartial and carried more impact. Widdicombe (1986: 223) recommended a review of its position, in view of its opposition to reform, and was also critical of the fact that a body which represents those who are the subject of investigation should play a major part in deciding the budget of the investigators. Lewis *et al.* (1986: 41) recommended that it be replaced with a body which included a substantial representation of consumer interests.

Since the demise of the Representative Body, the Commission submits the annual report to the local authority associations for their comments, but the Commission itself now arranges for the publication of the report. The Commission also meets the local authority associations every year, to discuss its business plan and the draft of the annual report. This is a more sensible practical arrangement from the LGO's point of view. The local authority associations can also comment on the allocation of funds to the LGO.

Every three years, the Commission has to report on its review of the operation of the 1974 Act (Section 23(12), as amended by Local Government Act 1988, Schedule 3). This report had to be presented to the Representative Body, but it is not entirely clear from the 1989 legislation what is now to happen to this report. In view of this, it appears that the report will be presented to the Secretary of State.

There are no plans to increase the remit of the Select Committee on the Parliamentary Commissioner, to include the LGO. Indeed, there has always been considerable constitutional hesitation in bringing aspects of local government directly under the supervision of Parliament in this way. Several of the world's national ombudsmen (for example, in Sweden, Denmark, Norway and France), who can examine complaints against local authorities, are responsible to their national parliaments, but there is no call to adopt such a system here.

GOOD ADMINISTRATIVE PRACTICE

As has been mentioned previously, the Commission has the aims of redressing injustice for individual complainants and improving administration.

Although these aims need not be mutually exclusive, there is some tension between them. They can result in a different relationship with local government, which may be happy to cooperate with individual grievance redress, but not so happy to see the local government ombudsmen having a roving commission to comment upon their procedures. Too much emphasis on the second role could mean that the Commission would become too much like management consultants.

Too much emphasis on grievance redress is also not without problems. The emphasis on informal settlements of complaints could lead to the situation where an individual complainant is satisfied at the expense of a thorough investigation of an authority's procedures. Although the LGO is unlikely to be compromised in this way, there is a recognition that an informal, speedy, local settlement could be better for an individual complainant than a printed report in six months time. Other potential complainants, who may be affected by the same poor procedures, would have to make their own complaints.

This is not perceived as a major problem, and Baroness Serota has said that the procedures are designed to support the 'traditional process of remedying grievances wherever possible within the democratic local government framework' (*CLA Annual Report* 1981–2: Foreword). Yardley (1983: 526), too, has emphasized the primary responsibility to the complainant:

> If a local settlement is reached which is agreeable to both the council and the complainant, and acceptable to the Local Ombudsman, there is nothing further which needs to be done on the issue in point, and it is unnecessary to draw further attention to the defect which has been discovered.

Despite the emphasis on grievance redress, the ombudsmen do attempt to improve procedures where possible, and have performed this function more satisfactorily than the PCA. The impressive record of the local government ombudsmen, not only in relation to securing redress for individual complainants but also in terms of encouraging good administrative practice, has been recognized by the government. The service 'has in practice proved a positive force for good, both by redressing individual grievances and by providing a spur to more responsive, efficient and fairer local administration' (Government Response to Widdicombe 1988: paras 6, 18). Indeed, it was suggested by the government that the LGO should take greater advantage of the opportunity in their reports to comment on the adequacy or otherwise of the procedures in individual authorities and to advise and comment on local authority procedures generally, using the wealth of experience they have gained through investigations (Government Response to Widdicombe 1988: 30–1).

The LGO's role has been extended, by the Local Government and Housing

Act 1989, which makes provisions for a wider and more assertive role. Section 22 of the Act amends Section 23 of the Local Government Act 1974, so that the Commission may, after consultation with the representative bodies and authorities concerned, provide appropriate advice and guidance about good administrative practice, and may also arrange for such guidance to be published. This gives statutory recognition of the valuable function already performed in this area.

The local authority associations believe that such advice should be given jointly by the Commission and the associations, as it would increase its effectiveness. The Commission supports the intention underlying this view, although it also considers that it has a right, under the Act, to publish advice without the support of the associations. It does expect, however, that normally such advice will be jointly published (*CLA Annual Report* 1990–1: 50). It may be that a Code of Good Administrative Practice for local authorities could be supplemented by a catalogue of common administrative errors, so that administrators could learn from the mistakes of others.

One response to this wider role has been the publication of a *Guide to the Local Government Ombudsman Service* (CLA 1990), compiled by the recently retired ombudsman, Mr Laws, and edited by him until July 1991, which will be developed and kept up-to-date. The present editor is Dr Yardley, and the Commission has arranged to update the *Guide* twice a year (*CLA Annual Report* 1991–2: 9). Work has also begun on the preparation of guidance notes for local authorities on the following topics: declaration of interests; disposal of land by local authorities; decoration following repair and improvement of council houses; and honouring undertakings (see *CLA Annual Report* 1990–1: 7). Guidance notes are also being prepared on council housing repairs. A booklet on devising a complaints system was published in 1992 (CLA 1992), and another document is being prepared in relation to good administrative practice, a draft of which has been sent to the local authority associations for consultation. A research and publications manager has been appointed to provide support work for the *Guide*, and to prepare guidance notes. There has also been an increase in the number of enquiries from local authorities about good practice that are not prompted by particular complaints or adverse findings. This is seen as indicating that councils are beginning to look at complaints and customer satisfaction 'from the angle of performance review, rather than as a series of embarrassing hiccoughs' (*CLA Annual Report* 1989–90: 30).

An additional power is given by Section 22 of the 1989 Act, which provides for the appointment of additional 'non-investigative', or advisory commissioners who could provide general advice to the Commissions on efficiency and good practice. These are expected to have backgrounds of an academic and financial character, but it has been decided not to implement this section at the present time. One role that they may perform when they are introduced, particularly if they include representatives of consumer organizations, would be to consider local authorities that do not implement the LGO's findings.

The LGO have encouraged the adoption of internal complaints proce-dures. In 1978, they published a code of practice in relation to complaints (CLA 1978), which has now been replaced by a new document on devising complaints procedures (CLA 1992). In addition, where faulty procedures have been found, they have, in many cases, tried to ensure that these have been improved. Although in the past practice in this area has been inconsis-tent, the situation is improving, and there are references in the results reports to actual improvements in procedures as a result of the investigation. For example, in one housing case (CLA case report 88/A/878) the ombudsman was pleased to note 'that the allocation system had been reorganised', so that 'such mistakes should not recur'. And in a case where there was a finding of poor judgement, but not maladministration (CLA case report 88/A/2144), the ombudsman said that he was 'pleased to see that new procedures have now been adopted which may help to avoid this happening in future'. In another case (CLA case report 88/A/647) the council had recognized that its system for administering grants was cumbersome, and had improved it.

Since 1990, the Commission, in its reports, has decided to publish its recommendations on the actions councils should take to remedy an injustice. In many cases this involves a recommendation in relation to the council's procedures. For example, in a housing case (CLA case report 89/A/1811), which revealed a 'catalogue of failures and omissions' resulting in a woman living in cold and damp conditions for six years, the council was asked to review and revise its procedures (*CLA Annual Report* 1990–1: 39). In another housing case (CLA case report 89/A/2963), as well as paying compensation to the complainant, the council was asked to review its housing allocation policy (*CLA Annual Report* 1990–1: 40). In two educa-tion cases (CLA case reports 89/C/341 and 89/C/1429), the councils concerned had improved procedures as a result of the investigations, in relation to the provision of free transport to school and to considering the adequacy of home tuition (*CLA Annual Report* 1990–1: 42).

There have been cases in the past where councils have been called upon to improve their procedures but how far this was monitored by the Commis-sion is not known. This situation may be improved by Section 26 of the Local Government and Housing Act 1989, which requires authorities to notify the local government ombudsmen of the steps taken to rectify administrative shortcomings. This provision certainly lends force to the argument that the local government ombudsmen ought to be playing a more effective role in overseeing administrative practice.

Baroness Serota, the first chair of the Commission in England, has said that there should be a Code of Good Administrative Practice (Serota

1983: 39), a suggestion which was also made by Justice (1971). Australia (Administration Decision (Judicial Review) Act 1977), and Sweden (Administrative Procedures Act 1971) have such practices, and indeed it has become a common feature of ombudsman systems that they do make recommendations for reforms and improvements. The newly introduced statutory duty of notification of steps taken to rectify procedures by a local authority, following the investigation of a complaint, reinforces the idea that the ombudsman is an overseer of good administration, and a document is now being prepared on the subject of good administrative practice.

The LGO acknowledge the value of using complaints to improve procedures, by noting that the settlement of one complaint can lead to a bad general practice being changed (*CLA Annual Report* 1990–1: 11), and they give examples of councils reviewing and changing practices as a result of investigations (p. 27). In a recent case (CLA case report 89/A/939), the LGO felt that the council had failed to conform to some basic standards of good administration in dealing with an application for housing, and they took the trouble to itemize in the annual report four basic axioms of good administration. These are, first, that

> although it is not wrong in itself for a council to discriminate for or against certain classes of applicants, such discrimination must be made for proper reasons and be seen to be fair. Second, that when allocating housing, and . . . when making many other decisions, proper criteria should be used. Third, that reasons should be given for administrative decisions; and, last, that such reasons should be noted in writing.
> (*CLA Annual Report* 1990–1: 14).

Not only are the ombudsmen encouraging good administrative practices, they are also making suggestions for legislative changes, where necessary, where a particular problem comes to light during the course of an investigation. One example is in relation to 'right to buy' cases, where the council does not have good title to the land in question (*CLA Annual Report* 1990–1: 6, 31). Another problem came to light in the case of certain owner-occupiers denied compensation when their homes were subject to a clearance order. The LGO mentioned a need for a change in the law to produce fair compensation for those who had not been owner-occupiers throughout the two years prior to a declaration of a clearance area. The legislation was amended to implement this (*CLA Annual Report* 1989–90: 8).

CONCLUSIONS

The LGO have been the most successful of the public sector ombudsmen. The Commission has a higher visibility and is studied and commented upon more frequently than the others. Its success is evidenced by the rising number of complaints, and it appears to be reaching those people who are powerless in society, as there is a rising number of complaints in relation to social services departments (*CLA Annual Report* 1989–90: 5). One reason why they may be more successful than the PCA is that recent governments have demanded more accountability from local than central government. In addition to this, successive ombudsmen have been bold and imaginative in their approach. In conclusion, it is fair to say that the impact of the LGO upon local government has been impressive, in relation to both securing redress for complainants and improving procedures within authorities.

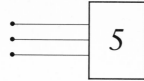

CONCLUSION

The world has witnessed the rapid growth of ombudsman systems in the past thirty years, with a proliferation of ombudsmen in both the public and private sectors. This growth was partly due to a recognition that the systems of control of public bodies were not adequate to deal with the increasingly complex post-war governments. Certainly, since the Second World War there have been movements towards both the protection of human rights and the protection of citizens against public bureaucracies (see Hayes 1991: 3). It was the latter that was of concern in Britain, and it has been said that our 'procedure for securing our personal freedom is efficient, but our procedure for preventing the abuse of power is not' (Denning 1949: 126). This growth is also partly a reflection of the increase in consumerism, and the fact that people are now prepared to challenge the decisions of public bodies.

Ombudsmen can trace their origins to the Swedish ombudsman introduced in the nineteenth century, although they are not a direct transplant, and it has been said that without openness, access to information 'and the general respect for democratic values inherent in Swedish culture, the ombudsman becomes a different and less effective animal' (Hayes 1991: 4). The public sector ombudsmen in Britain are, indeed, very different from their Scandinavian forebears.

The public sector ombudsmen in Britain are seven in number, and this book has looked at four of them: the three local government ombudsmen (LGO), and the Parliamentary Commissioner for Administration (PCA) and

Health Service Commissioner (HSC), who is the same person. It has not examined the local commissioners for Wales, Scotland or Northern Ireland. The PCA, HSC and LGO all have different remits, although the fact that the PCA and HSC are the same person has influenced their development along similar lines. Unlike the PCA and HSC, the LGO are removed from the Parliamentary context, and so they have developed differently. However, the pattern of the three services is essentially the same, and all have been very much influenced by the Parliamentary Commissioner Act 1967. It has been argued that the 1967 Act was unduly restrictive in its approach, with the result that our public sector ombudsmen are not as effective as they might have been. The 1967 Act, besides being a compromise, has operated outside a satisfactory context of adequate public law guarantees (see Lewis 1992: 19).

From their inception, the ombudsman arrangements in this country were subject to a great deal of adverse publicity. It is true that some of this was because people were mistaken about the extent of the ombudsman's powers in other countries, and therefore had unrealistic expectations of the institution. But there were justified criticisms; for example, in relation to access, to the narrow jurisdiction and to the fact that the institution had a civil service orientation. Despite this poor start, the PCA is now 'praised, in moderation, even by journalists, lawyers and academics' (Gregory and Pearson 1992: 471).

This is not to say that criticisms do not now exist, and one commentator has remarked that 'with the single exception of the Barlow Clowes affair, the standing of the Parliamentary Commissioner seems to have been particularly low during the later Thatcher years' (Bradley 1992: 356). Others have argued that one problem is that our ombudsman systems are seen as ancillary to the primary institutions for seeking justice, and it is doubtful if their full potential is being tapped (Lewis 1992: 74).

The PCA, HSC and LGO have been examined in turn in the preceding chapters and their strengths and weaknesses have been highlighted. In this concluding chapter it is proposed to turn from a description and discussion of the individual classical ombudsmen in Britain, and to look at the strengths and weaknesses of the system overall and some of the general issues affecting them all. It is important to bear in mind that although the office of the PCA was established some twenty-five years ago, the system as it stands is not sacrosanct, and perhaps this is the time to reconsider it in the light of experience of our own system and that of others (see Lewis 1992: 19).

THE OMBUDSMAN'S ROLE

Writing just after the introduction of the PCA, Rowat (1968: 292) described the ombudsman as 'an important new addition to the armoury of democratic government', predicting that 'the Ombudsman institution or its equivalent will become a standard part of the machinery of government throughout the democratic world.' Ombudsmen were established to investigate citizen complaints and provide redress for justified grievances. Unlike in some jurisdictions, however, the classical ombudsmen do not describe themselves as 'citizen's advocates' or 'people's champions'. They adopt a neutral and impartial position, acting neither on behalf of complainants nor for the authorities subject to investigation.

The PCA in office at the time of writing has said that his reports are not always 'comfortable to the Government', but neither are they always entirely comfortable to complainants because he is 'wholly dispassionate' in his approach (HC 158, 1992: Minutes of Evidence, 18 December 1991, Q. 66). Because he is impartial, he can vindicate departments when complaints are unfounded, in a way ministers cannot. Ombudsmen thus adopt an objective approach, which is incompatible with their being advocates. As Maloney (1983: 71) expresses it: 'He is not the citizen's lawyer for the simple reason that if his investigation vindicates the actions of the civil servant he must not hesitate to uphold him.'

On one level, therefore, ombudsmen are an alternative dispute-resolution mechanism. As such they provide a real alternative to the traditional justice system, given their wide powers of investigation, access to documents and independence. The courts, the traditional institution for dispute resolution, are not designed to review the facts or decide on the correct administrative decision. While tribunals are usually ideal for reviewing decisions, neither they nor the courts are equipped to investigate the *manner* in which the decision has been reached and find if there has been maladministration. Ombudsmen can fill this gap, and provide a remarkably effective alternative method to judicial review for rectifying maladministration (Woolf 1990: 91).

Another advantage of ombudsmen is the fact that they can rove broadly across the activities of those authorities subject to their jurisdiction. This external review can bring a different light to bear on particular decisions and procedures (see Lewis 1992: 69). Certainly, the PCA has in 'the twenty-five years of its existence . . . clearly established itself as a valuable addition to the apparatus of complaint-handling mechanisms available to United Kingdom citizens' (Gregory and Pearson 1992: 484). The same can be said of the other classical ombudsmen.

Ombudsmen are one among a number of methods of controlling public bodies and one form of accountability mechanism available to the citizen.

Ombudsmen must not be seen in isolation, and their relation to other bodies is important. There have been calls for an integrated system of control mechanisms to protect citizens fully from abuse of administrative power (see Woolf 1990: 92). Thus, there is a need to foster partnership between judicial and non-judicial review; the courts, the ombudsman and tribunals should each have the power in appropriate cases to refer questions for determination to the appropriate body (Woolf 1990: 113). The functions and jurisdiction of the courts, tribunals and ombudsmen are not immutable, and the 'proper divide between the jurisdiction of the courts, tribunals and the ombudsman must be defined and redefined as circumstances change' (Woolf 1990: 123).

All the public sector ombudsmen are concerned with injustice caused as a result of maladministration, and these concepts have been explored in the preceding chapters. Sir Edmund Compton, the first PCA, remarked that 'Nobody can define maladministration in plain terms' (HC 350, 1968: Minutes of Evidence, Q. 151), and there is still some truth in this. Maladministration is not defined in any of the legislation, and it has been left to the ombudsmen to develop the concept over the years. One issue of central concern is whether the concepts of maladministration and injustice are too restrictive. It is only in the UK, among all the ombudsmen in developed countries, that the ombudsmen are confined to investigating cases of maladministration. Others have powers either to look at unreasonable action by public authorities or to report on failures in the public service (see Stacey 1978: 231).

Some have argued that this is too restrictive, and Justice (1977: para. 19) proposed that the PCA should no longer be limited to investigating complaints about maladministration, recognizing that the British ombudsman was more restricted than any other in this respect. More recently, Justice (1988: 138) has decided that the term is flexible enough, and has decided that no change is needed in the wording of the statute to widen the powers of the ombudsman. However, there are others who still believe that legislation to change the jurisdictional definition is desirable, maintaining that the concept of maladministration has not been very broadly developed (Lewis 1992: 41–2). Justice (1988: 138) also thought it unnecessary to amend the phrase 'injustice' in consequence of maladministration, believing that 'injustice' was sufficiently flexible and wide ranging. It has, however, been argued that the requirement that there has to be a finding of injustice before any remedial action can be taken should be removed. This would have the effect of directing the ombudsman to adopt a central concern with the adequacy of procedures (Lewis 1992: 5).

The Whyatt Report (Justice 1961), which was fairly conservative in its recommendations, is largely responsible for confining the PCA, and thus the other public sector ombudsmen, to investigating alleged maladministration. However, the report had also recommended the setting up of a comprehensive system of administrative tribunals, including a tribunal with general jurisdiction. In the absence of this, there is no system for a general appeal on the merits of administrative decisions. This is a serious drawback, and one which was recognized many years ago by Lord Denning (1949: 80), when he noted that although we have a number of tribunals, there is no general administrative court. Perhaps if we had a system of administrative courts, confining the PCA to maladministration might have been more justifiable. As it stands, we have no system for a general appeal on the merits of decisions and our ombudsmen cannot look at the exercise of discretion taken without maladministration. Nor would a system of administrative courts make the ombudsman irrelevant. Sweden and Finland have administrative courts, together with ombudsmen. They are complementary to each other, not alternatives (see Rowat 1968: 222).

EFFECTIVENESS OF THE OMBUDSMEN

In the introductory chapter some criteria that may be used to assess the effectiveness of ombudsmen were examined. The effectiveness of each of the public sector ombudsmen has been referred to in the preceding chapters, and what is proposed here is to make some general points. In order to be effective, ombudsmen need to have wide powers of investigation, and in this respect the English public sector ombudsmen score highly. Not only does the legislation give them extensive powers to enable them to acquire all the necessary information, but their working practices have meant that the thoroughness of their investigations cannot be faulted.

Where their effectiveness can be criticized is in relation to jurisdictional coverage. I do not wish to repeat the discussions of the preceding chapters, but many of the statutory exclusions of jurisdiction cannot be justified, and there have been numerous calls for their abolition and an extension of the ombudsmen's remits. Indeed, the general principle should be that the broadest possible jurisdiction should be encouraged, except where a clear case for exclusion exists. This would mean that all administrative action would be subject to scrutiny, in the absence of clear reasons for exclusion. Jurisdictional matters need to be kept under review, and there needs to be systematic examination in the light of the increased 'contracting out' of public services and privatization of public affairs (see Lewis 1992: 6).

The ombudsmen should also be given the power to conduct investigations on their own initiative. In this respect, the UK ombudsmen are out of line with most other systems, the only other ombudsmen not having this power being the French, German Federal Petitions Committee and those of Leichtenstein and the City of Zurich (Haller 1988: 40). Such a power is not likely to be extensively used, in particular because of resource constraints, but it would allow the ombudsmen to investigate when, for example, they had reason to believe that a particular section of a department or authority was not dealing properly with its business.

All our ombudsmen receive fairly low numbers of complaints and investigate very few cases. In this respect, the LGO have a better record than the other two. There is no doubt that the ombudsmen could be more extensively used. However, it has been argued that the problem is not one of just increasing the workload, as there would be little point in bringing complaints that could be solved elsewhere. There is also the danger that a larger caseload could mean that complaints were no longer investigated with the same thoroughness, which might jeopardize the 'quality control' side of the ombudsmen's work (Gregory and Pearson 1992: 485). This need not necessarily happen, and it has been argued that there may be some benefit in having a two-tier method of investigation (see Chapter 2).

There are improvements which could be made to make the ombudsmen more accessible and to increase public awareness. Unlike those to the LGO and HSC, complaints to the PCA are filtered through MPs. Not only is the PCA out of line with the other public sector ombudsmen in this respect, but it is out of line with ombudsmen worldwide. France is the only other jurisdiction where it is not permitted to take a complaint directly to the ombudsman (Stacey 1978: 231). This filter could account for the very low numbers of complaints the PCA receives.

The arguments relating to this have been discussed at length in Chapter 2. There are some who wish to maintain the filter, including the Select Committee, and it has been argued that it would be unwise to weaken the links between the PCA and MPs and Parliament, because these 'links give authority and status to investigations and assist in achieving the effective implementation of any recommendation which is made' (Woolf 1990: 88). It is felt that the LGO do not have the same support as the PCA, and that this explains the much less satisfactory record of their recommendations being implemented. However, there is a belief that the member filter does deter complainants, and Justice (1988), among others, has called for direct access. Like Woolf (1990), Justice is 'firmly convinced that the work of the PCA gains much strength from his links with Parliament' (Justice 1988: 88), and would wish to see this preserved. However, Justice believes that the link could be preserved in a number of ways. First, MPs would still be entitled to refer cases. The PCA should also inform the Select Committee about his or her investigations. In addition, if the PCA believes, on the basis of individual complaints, that a particular branch of a department is not dealing with its business properly, then subject to Select Committee approval the PCA should be able to carry out systematic investigation of the work of that branch (Justice 1988: 138). If this procedure were adopted, direct access would not involve a severance of the links with MPs and Parliament.

Direct access may make it easier for citizens to bring complaints, but in addition the visibility of the public sector ombudsmen needs to be raised. There is still widespread ignorance of the various ombudsmen. A recent survey by the Office of Fair Trading revealed that, when prompted, 27 per cent of consumers were aware of the Insurance Ombudsman, 24 per cent of the Banking Ombudsman and 22 per cent of the Building Societies Ombudsman. The survey notes that these figures are almost certainly over-estimates (OFT 1991: 57). Although the survey only deals with the private sector ombudsmen, such a lack of awareness suggests that much of the population is probably ignorant of the work of the public sector ombudsmen too.

Bradley (1992: 355) notes that for most of the past twenty-five years the PCA has 'failed to achieve any real place in the public's understanding'. The 1991 annual report has photographs of past and present staff, but it is questionable whether this goes far enough 'to remedy the inability of the general public . . . to attach a human face to the Ombudsman' (Bradley 1992: 355). Justice (1988: 137) notes that there have been considerable efforts by the PCA and LGO in relation to publicity, but there is still much to be done, and members of the legal profession are called upon 'to be well informed about the assistance which an ombudsman may be able to give to their clients'. Improvements need to be made in the way the press report the ombudsman's decisions. Ombudsmen could become involved in 'outreach' work and more vigorous advertising. Some thought could be given to the possibility of regional offices.

Ombudsmen should be able to ensure that adequate remedies are available where maladministration is found. According to Justice (1988: 85), it is the specific function of ombudsmen to determine whether an aggrieved individual has suffered unjustly from the defective working of the administrative machinery, and if so to ensure that an adequate remedy is provided by the authority concerned. The PCA, HSC and LGO can only recommend a remedy, and they do not make legally binding decisions. This, in itself, does not mean that they cannot provide an adequate remedy, and is in line with the powers of other ombudsmen worldwide.

Ombudsmen not only recommend financial remedies, but also ask that decisions be reconsidered and that faulty procedures be rectified. This is unlike the private sector, where the ombudsmen take the view that only a financial loss is capable of compensation. Ombudsmen in the private sector emphasize the supervisory or policing role they perform and suggest that it is this role and not the quasi-judicial role that makes them effective. The existence of the office is a deterrent in itself (see Meriden 1991: 43). In some cases the remedies available to the public sector ombudsmen are better than the courts, in that ombudsmen can give compensation where the courts would have no power to award damages.

This is not to suggest that the area of remedies is unproblematic. While the PCA and HSC generally have no problem in persuading departments and authorities to give the remedy recommended, the LGO's record is marred by the number of authorities that have, over the years, refused to follow the LGO's recommendation. This poor record on enforcement has led to a number of calls for court enforcement. As was suggested in Chapter 4, this is not necessarily the solution to the problem.

The topic of remedies must also be seen in the context of the concepts of maladministration and injustice, as it is only where injustice is found as a consequence of maladministration that a remedy will be forthcoming. It has been suggested that these two concepts cannot be separated because every maladministration results in injustice in that there is a breach of the citizen's right to good government. However, even if this is accepted, it is thought that there is no obvious remedy to compensate for the loss of good government and it is not susceptible to a settlement (see Meriden 1991: 43).

Another major problem with all the ombudsmen is the time taken for investigations. Indeed, recent research indicates that the length of time taken by the PCA to complete investigations was the main reason why MPs were dissatisfied with the office (see Drewry and Harlow 1990). All the ombudsmen are making efforts to improve their record in this respect, but there are limitations, given the thoroughness with which investigations are conducted.

In order to be effective, an ombudsman must be seen to be impartial and independent. In this respect it may be better if the PCA and his staff were drawn from a wider pool than the civil service. The LGO are better in this respect, drawing their staff from a wider pool than local authorities.

GOOD ADMINISTRATIVE PRACTICE

Although all the ombudsmen have the primary task of investigating complaints about action or inaction alleged to have led to injustice for the complainant, they also perform an external auditing function. The present PCA has said that, while it is a good thing to produce redress for a wronged individual, it is even better if he can 'suggest or encourage a change of procedures or systems by the organisation complained against, which will diminish the chance of the circumstances which led to the complaint recurring' (Reid 1992: 6). The LGO have, as their main objective, the investigation of complaints with a view to securing, where appropriate, both redress for the complainant and better administration. Their supporting objectives include the issuing of guidance on good administrative practice.

It has been argued that there has always been a tension in British ombudsman systems between the function of redressing injustice for the individual and improving administration (Lewis 1992: 19). The LGO has performed the latter function much more satisfactorily than the PCA. This is not to say that the PCA has not produced improvements in administration, but the circumstances in which this occurs are somewhat unpredictable and unpatterned (Lewis 1992: 45).

Justice (1988: 6–22) recommended an updated and comprehensive set of non-statutory 'principles of good administration' to which the public and all administrators would have access. Such codes of practice, Justice believes, would be best drawn up by the ombudsmen. However, doubts have been expressed as to whether all the ombudsmen would accept this. Lee (1991: 20) suspects that 'the PCA might be less than enthusiastic about his nomination for this task', as some ombudsmen might argue that their job is to identify maladministration, not to pontificate on good administration. Indeed, it has been argued that the ombudsmen offices were not set up with the purpose of formulating and issuing advice, and it is not an ombudsman's function to engage in such activity. Such codes of practice, it is said, would come more appropriately from other bodies. Service providers can, and do, learn lessons from decided cases and issue instructions to their own staff on the basis of them.

On the other hand, some argue that ombudsmen should take a lead in setting out the principles of good administration, and that it would be useful if ombudsmen played a part in helping to prevent problems arising in future as well as investigating after they have occurred (Meriden 1991: 31). Guidance of this sort is a by-product of individual decisions, and a code could act as a broader method of securing the avoidance of injustice. Ombudsmen in other jurisdictions are proactive. For example, the New Zealand ombudsman has produced a code of good practice. Within Britain, the Audit Commission is not inhibited about giving advice. It is thought that ombudsmen should have confidence in what can be demonstrated by their own experience (Meriden 1991: 32). As was discussed in Chapter 4, the LGO are involved in drawing up such codes. In the private sector, the ombudsmen for the banks and building societies are consulted on the revision of the banking code of practice.

Codes of good administrative practice would go some way to reforming the system of public law. They could embody, among other things, a duty to give reasons for decisions, which imposes a healthy discipline in the decision maker. Such a duty also helps to ensure that decisions are better thought out, and acts as a check on arbitrary decision making. Woolf (1990: 92) thought that the introduction of a general requirement that reasons should normally be available, at least on request, for all administrative actions was the 'most beneficial improvement which could be made to English administrative law'.

Wheare (1973: 2) believes that we should seek the principles of good administration and embody them in the organization and training of civil servants. In addition to this, public administrators must improve their communication skills, listen to the public, minimize delay, give reasons for their actions and concede that appeals and decisions on complaints are. openly fairer when decided by an agency external to the one against which the complaint lies (Reid 1992: 6).

Another reform, recommended by Justice (1988: 22), was the establishment of an administrative review commission, perhaps based on the Council on Tribunals. This would be independent of government, and would be charged with the duty of overseeing all aspects of administrative justice and drawing attention to defects and proposing reforms. Similar proposals for the reform of administrative law were made by Social Democratic Party lawyers (SDP 1983). A single Commission for Public Administration was advocated, which would combine the existing ombudsmen offices and include jurisdiction over complaints about government contracting, the judicial system and certain public corporations. Harden and Lewis (1986) have suggested that a standing administrative conference be established (p. 307), and also that an Administrative Procedure Act be enacted, which would be designed to produce open discussion, natural justice and rational planning processes (p. 255).

THE CITIZEN'S CHARTER

The role of the ombudsmen in the Citizen's Charter movement is of interest. The Citizen's Charter has been described as an affirmation by government of the right of the citizen as a consumer to expect proper standards of public services and to be compensated in the event of a failure (Hayes 1991: 14). Such an objective is one that most ombudsmen would support. However, the Charter itself makes only very brief references to the PCA and HSC. The Select Committee, aware of the relevance of the Charter for the work of the ombudsman, looked at its implications. The Select Committee was told that when the Charter was published, the Secretary of the Cabinet wrote to the PCA saying that there were no proposals to change his powers or jurisdiction and that this reflected a wish to avoid tinkering with 'a machine that works well as it is' (HC 158, 1992: Appendix to Minutes of Evidence, 2).

It is strange that the ombudsmen are not at the forefront of this development. Bradley (1992: 356) suggests that a reason for this is that the government may not welcome 'the potential contribution that a more flexible and responsive model of the existing Ombudsman could make to meeting the citizens' expectations'. He believes that the government is ambivalent about the ombudsman. The Citizen's Charter speaks about the introduction of 'new forms of redress where these can be made to stimulate rather than distract from efficiency' (White Paper 1991: 5), and about the need within the public services 'to increase both choice and competition' (p. 4). Bradley (1992: 357) queries whether this is a veiled criticism of the ombudsman system.

The Charter sets performance targets for the public services, and departmental charters are to state what levels of service citizens can expect. There seem to be different views about whether charters should have 'quality auditors' built in or not, but what has not been properly addressed is how far there may be overlap between such ideas and the potential of our existing ombudsmen, were they to be invested with similar powers to their overseas counterparts (see Lewis 1992: 74). There must be some independent procedure that monitors actual output, and this would seem to be a task for the ombudsman, using consumer complaints for monitoring purposes. Certainly, the Citizen's Charter should not make the ombudsmen redundant in the public sector, and ombudsmen should be at the forefront of any developments in this area.

The Citizen's Charter speaks about the need to increase both choice and competition within the public services (White Paper 1991: 4). One way of achieving this has been to change the method of delivery of these services. In particular, private organizations have been contracted by government to perform functions that used to be performed by public bodies. This 'marketization' of services has consequences for ombudsmen, as their jurisdiction covers public bodies.

The present Parliamentary Commissioner feels that his jurisdiction extends to cases of maladministration by private sector contractors carrying out work done previously by government departments. Section 5 of the Parliamentary Commissioner Act 1967 provides that the ombudsman can investigate administrative actions carried out *by* and *on behalf of* the government departments and other public sector bodies listed in Schedule 2 of the Act. If cases do arise involving private contractors, the ombudsman feels that 'Departments and Agencies should retain and sustain responsibility for standards of service provided to the citizen' (*PCA Annual Report* 1992: 2).

Whatever system for delivery of public services is adopted, there should still be an effective method of redress for grievances. While the emphasis placed on the importance of having effective internal systems for handling complaints is to be applauded, external mechanisms are needed too, if complainants are to have confidence in the system. Ombudsmen are ideally placed to perform this external redress function.

A SINGLE OMBUDSMAN SYSTEM

One reform that has been suggested is to have a single ombudsman system for the public sector ombudsmen, bringing together the existing three public sector ombudsman systems (see Lewis 1992: 72). It was recognized some years ago that the wide array of ombudsmen can cause confusion (Williams 1976: 5), and Sir Alan Marre recognized that in the long term there would need to be a consideration of how a more coordinated total system, more directly related to the interests of members of the public, could be brought about (*PCA Annual Report* 1975).

This matter was examined by the Select Committee (see HC 254, 1980), but no definite proposals for reorganizing the present arrangements were made. Justice (1988) discussed the suggestion for an integrated service, under which all the ombudsmen would operate under the same legislation, but decided against recommending the creation of a single integrated service. It was, however, urged that the closest possible cooperation between ombudsmen should continue to be maintained, and efforts be made between the PCA and LGO to ensure that complaints reached their appropriate destination (pp. 136–7). As it was noted that the existing arrangements for composite investigations were working satisfactorily, it was decided that no case was made out for an integrated service, and no proposals were made for this (p. 40).

However, there is no doubt that confusion is sown in the minds of the public by the separate sets of offices and jurisdictions. Each ombudsman attempts to funnel on the complaints which are inappropriately channelled, but many complaints may get lost in the system. An integrated system, sharing the same facilities, would mean that there was one port of call for complainants. Hayes (1991: 13) has called for a one-stop ombudsman office with sub-divisions, or even a willingness of ombudsmen to reroute complaints to an appropriate colleague without undue formality.

Although there seems to be little current pressure in Britain for a single ombudsman system, perhaps the proposal ought to be re-examined, and ways sought to reduce the confusion in the minds of the public about the different jurisdictions of the ombudsmen. The recently formed UK Ombudsman Association may improve public awareness of ombudsmen, and help dispel the confusion about their different remits.

CONCLUSION

It has been argued that the presence of the ombudsmen has increased public confidence in public administration, provided a means of rectifying administrative errors and succeeded to some extent in humanizing the bureaucracy.

The existence of ombudsmen is symbolic of a governmental desire that government should be well conducted and citizens well treated, and this has a cautionary effect on officials (Hayes 1991: 7). Despite these undoubted achievements, it must be said that few institutions 'work so well that they cannot be improved' (Gregory and Pearson 1992: 48).

Generally the public sector ombudsmen have been criticized because of the widespread ignorance among the public of what they are and what they do, the small numbers of people who take advantage of their existence and their limited remit. It has been said that they err on the side of caution, and that the PCA is 'still suffering from the undue caution of the 1967 scheme and the remarkably effective way in which the Sir Humphreys of the 1960s insulated the Ombudsman from the public that he or she should serve' (Bradley 1992: 354). Indeed, it has been said that the PCA is by most yardsticks less effective than the ombudsman systems in operation elsewhere (Lewis 1992: 57), and the least effective of the public sector ombudsmen in the UK.

Despite these criticisms, the growing popularity of the concept is evident from ombudsmen's spread from the public sector to the private sector, and from the fact that a European Ombudsman is to be appointed. Ombudsmen are here to stay, but it is doubtful if their full potential is being tapped (Lewis 1992: 74), and now would be an opportune time for a radical re-examination of their role. This re-examination must take place within the context of reform of our entire system of public law, with the relative strengths and weaknesses of ombudsmen, courts, tribunals and other institutions being assessed (Lewis 1992: 47). In particular, the role of ombudsmen in relation to the adequacy of procedures needs developing. There is a need for general oversight of administrative procedures within public life (Lewis 1992: 68). The ombudsmen are ideally placed to fulfil this role.

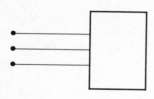

APPENDIX 1: GOVERNMENT DEPARTMENTS AND OTHER BODIES SUBJECT TO INVESTIGATION BY THE PARLIAMENTARY COMMISSIONER FOR ADMINISTRATION

Advisory, Conciliation and Arbitration Service
Agricultural Wages Committee
Ministry of Agriculture, Fisheries and Food
Arts Council of Great Britain
British Council
British Library Board
Building Societies Commission
Certification Officer
The Central Statistical Office of the Chancellor of the Exchequer
Charity Commission
Office of the Minister for the Civil Service
Civil Service Commission
Co-operative Development Agency
Countryside Commission
Countryside Council for Wales
Crafts Council
Crofters Commission

Crown Estate Office
Customs and Excise
Data Protection Registrar
Ministry of Defence
Development Commission
Education Assets Board
Department for Education
Central Bureau for Educational Visits and Exchanges
Office of the Director General of Electricity Supply
Department of Employment
Department of the Environment
English Heritage
Equal Opportunities Commission
Export Credits Guarantee Department
Office of the Director General of Fair Trading
British Film Institute
Foreign and Commonwealth Office
Forestry Commission
Registry of Friendly Societies
Office of the Director General of Gas Supply
Department of Health
Health and Safety Commission
Health and Safety Executive
Home Office
Horserace Betting Levy Board
Housing Corporation
Housing for Wales
The Human Fertilisation and Embryology Authority
Central Office of Information
Inland Revenue
Intervention Board for Agricultural Produce
Land Registry
Legal Aid Board
Scottish Legal Aid Board
The following general lighthouse authorities: (a) the Corporation of the Trinity
    House of Deptford Strond; (b) the Commissioners of Northern Lighthouses
Lord Chancellor's Department
Lord President of the Council's Office
Medical Practices Committee
Scottish Medical Practices Committee
Museums and Galleries Commission
National Debt Office
Department of National Heritage
Trustees of the National Heritage Memorial Fund
Department for National Savings
Nature Conservancy Council for England

Commission for the New Towns
Development Corporations for New Towns
Northern Ireland Court Service
Northern Ireland Office
Ordnance Survey
Office of Population Censuses and Surveys
Registrar of Public Lending Right
Office of Public Service and Science
Public Record Office
Scottish Record Office
Commission for Racial Equality
Red Deer Commission
Department of the Registrars of Scotland
General Register Office, Scotland
Agricultural and Food Research Council
Economic and Social Research Council
Medical Research Council
Natural Environment Research Council
Science and Engineering Research Council
Residuary Bodies
Office of the Commissioner for the Rights of Trade Union Members
Royal Mint
Scottish Courts Administration
Scottish Office
Department of Social Security
Central Council for Education and Training in Social Work
Sports Council
Scottish Natural Heritage
Scottish Sports Council
Sports Council for Wales
Office for Standards in Education
Stationery Office
Office of the Director General of Telecommunications
English Tourist Board
Scottish Tourist Board
Wales Tourist Board
Board of Trade
Department of Trade and Industry
Traffic Director for London
Agricultural Training Board
Clothing and Allied Products Industry Training Board
Construction Industry Training Board
Engineering Industry Training Board
Hotel and Catering Industry Training Board
Plastics Processing Industry Training Board
Road Transport Industry Training Board
Department of Transport

Treasury
Treasury Solicitor
Urban development corporations
Development Board for Rural Wales
Office of the Director General of Water Services
Welsh Office

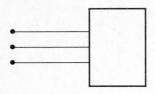

APPENDIX 2: ADDRESSES OF THE PUBLIC SECTOR OMBUDSMEN

The Parliamentary Commissioner for Administration
Church House
Great Smith Street
London SW1P 3BW
Telephone: 071–276 2130

The Health Service Commissioner for England
Church House
Great Smith Street
London SW1P 3BW
Telephone: 071–276 2035 or 071–276 3000

The Local Government Ombudsmen
21 Queen Anne's Gate
London SW1H 9BY
Telephone: 071–222 5622

Beverley House
17 Shipton Road
York YO3 6FZ
Telephone: 0904 630151/2/3

The Oaks
Westwood Way
Westwood Business Park
Coventry CV4 8JB
Telephone: 0203 695999

Office of the Northern Ireland Commissioner for Complaints
33 Wellington Place
Belfast BT1 6HN
Telephone: 0232 233821

Commission for Local Administration in Scotland
5 Shandwick Place
Edinburgh EH2 4RG
Telephone: 031–229 4472

Commission for Local Administration in Wales
Derwen House
Court Road
Bridgend
Mid Glamorgan CF31 1BN
Telephone: 0656 661235/6

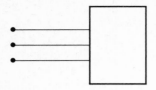

BIBLIOGRAPHY

Barron, A. and Scott, C. (1992) The Citizen's Charter Programme, *Modern Law Review*, 55, 526.

Bell, C. and Vaughan, J.W. (1988). The Building Societies Ombudsman: a customers champion?, *Solicitors Journal*, 132, 1478.

Birkinshaw, P. (1985) *Grievances, Remedies and the State*. London, Sweet and Maxwell.

Bradley, A.W. (1992) Sachsenhausen, Barlow Clowes – and then, *Public Law*, 353.

Bratton, K. (1984) The Work of the Commissioner for Local Administration in Scotland 1975–1983, Occasional Paper Number 25. Edmonton, University of Alberta, International Ombudsman Institute.

Caiden, G. (1988) The challenge of change, *Fourth International Ombudsman Conference Papers*, Canberra, 1.

CLA (1978) *Code of Practice for Complaints Procedures*. Jointly issued by the Commission for Local Administration, the Representative Body and the Local Authority Associations. London, Commission for Local Administration.

CLA (1990) *Guide to the Local Government Ombudsman Service*. London, Longman.

CLA (1992) *Devising a Complaints System, Guidance on Good Practice No. 1*. London, Commission for Local Administration.

Clark, D. (1984) The citizen and the administrator in France – the conseil d'etat versus ombudsman debate revisited, *Public Administration* 62, 161.

Clothier, C. (1984) Legal problems of an ombudsman, *Law Society Gazette*, 81, 3108.

Clothier, C. (1986) The value of an ombudsman, *Public Law*, 204.

Commonwealth Ombudsman (1983–4) *Annual Report 1983–84*. Canberra, Commonwealth Ombudsman.

Crawford, C. (1988) Complaints, codes and ombudsmen in local government', *Public Law*, 246.

Denning, A. (1949) *Freedom under the Law*. London, Stevens.

Department of the Environment (1990) *National Code of Local Government Conduct*. DoE Circular 8/90. London, DoE.

Drewry, G. and Harlow, C. (1990) A cutting edge? The Parliamentary Commissioner and MPs, *Modern Law Review*, 53, 745.

ECG Briefing Paper (1990) *A Briefing Paper from the European Community Group, August 1990*. London, ECG.

Farleigh Report (1971). *Report of the Farleigh Hospital Committee of Inquiry*, Cmnd 4557. London, HMSO.

Franks (1957) *Report of the Committee on Administrative Tribunals and Inquiries*, Cmnd 218. London, HMSO.

Friedmann, K. (1988) Realisation of ombudsman recommendations, *Fourth International Ombudsman Conference Papers*, Canberra, 105.

Gellhorn, W. (1967) *Ombudsmen and Others*. Cambridge, MA, Harvard University Press.

Giddings, P. and Pearson, J. (1991) The health service commissioner: some research issues, Political Studies Association Conference paper, Lancaster.

Government Observations (1979) *Observations by the Government on the Fourth Report from the Select Committee on the Parliamentary Commissioner for Administration, Review of Access and Jurisdiction Session 1977–78*, Cmnd 7449. London, HMSO.

Government Response to Widdicombe (1988) *The Conduct of Local Authority Business. The Government Response to the Report of the Widdicombe Committee*, Cm 433. London, HMSO.

Gregory, R. and Alexander, A. (1973) Our Parliamentary Ombudsman (Part II), *Public Administration*, 51, 48.

Gregory, R. and Hutchesson, P. (1975) *The Parliamentary Ombudsman*. London, George Allen and Unwin.

Gregory, R. and Pearson, J. (1992) The Parliamentary Ombudsman after twenty-five years: problems and solutions, *Public Administration*, 70, 469.

Gwyn, W. (1982) The Ombudsman in Britain: a qualified success in government reform, *Public Administration*, 60, 177.

Haller, W. (1988). The place of the ombudsman in the world community, *Fourth International Ombudsman Conference Papers*, Canberra, 29.

Harden, I. and Lewis, N. (1986) *The Noble Lie*. London, Hutchinson.

Harlow, C. (1978) Ombudsmen in search of a role, *Modern Law Review*, 41, 446.

Harlow, C. and Rawlings, R. (1984) *Law and Administration*. London, Weidenfeld and Nicolson.

Hayes, M. (1991) Emerging issues for ombudsmen, United Kingdom Ombudsman Conference paper, Meriden.

HC 44 (1992) *Report from the Select Committee on the Parliamentary Commissioner for Administration. Session 1991–92.* London, HMSO.

HC 45 (1978) *First Report from the Select Committee on the Parliamentary Commissioner for Administration: Independent Review of Hospital Complaints in the National Health Service. Session 1977–78.* London, HMSO.

HC 129 (1991) *First Report from the Select Committee on the Parliamentary Commissioner for Administration: Report of the Parliamentary Commissioner for Administration for 1989. Session 1990–91.* London, HMSO.

HC 148 (1981) *Second Report from the Select Committee on the Parliamentary Commissioner for Administration: Parliamentary Commissioner for Administration Annual Report for 1980. Session 1980–81.* London, HMSO.

HC 158 (1992) *Second Report from the Select Committee on the Parliamentary Commissioner for Administration: the Implications of the Citizen's Charter for the Work of the Parliamentary Commissioner for Administration. Session 1991–92,* London, HMSO.

HC 182 (1991) *Annual Report of the Northern Ireland Parliamentary Commissioner for Administration and Commissioner for Complaints for 1991.* London, HMSO.

HC 254 (1980) *Second Report of the Select Committee on the Parliamentary Commissioner for Administration: the System of Ombudsmen in the United Kingdom. Session 1979–80.* London, HMSO.

HC 258 (1982) *Second Report for Session 1981–82: Parliamentary Commissioner for Administration Annual Report for 1981. Session 1981–82.* London, HMSO.

HC 282 (1976) *First Report from the Select Committee on the Parliamentary Commissioner for Administration: Reports of the Health Service Commissioner for 1974–75. Session 1975–76.* London, HMSO.

HC 322 (1984) *Fifth Report for Session 1983–84: Parliamentary Commissioner for Administration Annual Report for 1983. Session 1983–84.* London, HMSO.

HC 347 (1992) *Second Report for Session 1991–92. Annual Report for the Parliamentary Commissioner for Administration for 1991.* London, HMSO.

HC 350 (1968) *Second Report from the Select Committee on the Parliamentary Commissioner for Administration. Session 1967–68.* London, HMSO.

HC 353 (1990) *Third Report from the Select Committee on the Parliamentary Commissioner for Administration: Report of the Parliamentary Commissioner for Administration for 1989. Session 1989–90.* London, HMSO.

HC 368 (1991) *Fourth Report from the Select Committee on the Parliamentary Commissioner for Administration: Report of the Parliamentary Commissioner for Administration for 1990. Session 1990–91.* London, HMSO.

HC 385 (1969) *Second Report from the Select Committee on the Parliamentary Commissioner for Administration. Session 1968–69.* London, HMSO.

HC 419 (1982) *Third Report for Session 1981–82: Annual Report for the Health Service Commissioner for 1981–82. Session 1981–82.* London, HMSO.

HC 433 (1989) *Second Report from the Select Committee on the Parliamentary Commissioner for Administration: Reports of the Health Service Commissioner for 1987–88. Session 1988–89.* London, HMSO.

HC 441 (1990) *Second Report from the Select Committee on the Parliamentary*

Commissioner for Administration: Reports of the Health Service Commissioner for 1989. Session 1989–90. London, HMSO.

HC 448 (1986) *Third Report from the Select Committee on the Parliamentary Commissioner for Administration: Local Government Cases: Enforcement of Remedies. Session 1985–86.* London, HMSO.

HC 498 (1975) *Fifth Report of the Parliamentary Commissioner for Administration. Session 1974–75.* London, HMSO.

HC 569 (1993) *Fifth Report for Session 1992–93. Annual Report for the Parliamentary Commissioner for Administration for 1992.* London, HMSO.

HC 615 (1978) *Fourth Report from the Select Committee on the Parliamentary Commissioner for Administration: Review of Access and Jurisdiction. Session 1977–78.* London, HMSO.

HC 619 (1984) *Fourth Report of the Select Committee on the Parliamentary Commissioner for Administration. Session 1983–84.* London, HMSO.

HC 650 (1993) *Report of the Select Committee on the Parliamentary Commissioner for Administration: the Powers, Work and Jurisdiction of the Ombudsman. Session 1992–93.* London, HMSO.

Hill, L. (1976) *The Model Ombudsman: Institutionalizing New Zealand's Democratic Experiment.* Princeton, NJ, Princeton University Press.

Himsworth, C. (1986) Parliamentary teeth for local ombudsmen?, *Public Law*, 546.

Justice (1961) *The Citizen and the Administration: the Redress of Grievances (the Whyatt Report).* London, Stevens.

Justice (1969) *The Citizen and his Council: Ombudsmen for Local Government?* London, Stevens.

Justice (1971) *Administration under Law: a Report by Justice.* London, Stevens.

Justice (1977) *Our Fettered Ombudsman.* London, Justice.

Justice (1980) *The Local Ombudsman: a Review of the First Five Years.* London, Justice.

Justice (1988) *Administrative Justice: Some Necessary Reforms. Report of the Committee of the Justice–All Souls Review of Administrative Law in the United Kingdom.* Oxford, Clarendon Press.

Labour Party (1964) *Let's Go with Labour for a New Britain. Manifesto for the 1964 General Election.* London, The Labour Party.

Lee, S. (1991) Ombudsmen over all our shoulders, United Kingdom Ombudsman Conference paper, Meriden.

Lewis, N. (1979). The case for change in the ombudsman service, *Municipal and Public Services Journal*, 8 January, 597.

Lewis, N. (1992) *The Classical Ombudsmen.* University of Sheffield, Centre for Socio-Legal Studies (unpublished).

Lewis, N., Seneviratne, M. and Cracknell, S. (1986) *Complaints Procedures in Local Government.* University of Sheffield, Centre for Criminological and Socio-Legal Studies.

Longley, D. (1993) *Public Law and Health Service Accountability.* Buckingham, Open University Press.

Maloney, M. (1983) The ombudsman as mediator, reformer and fighter?, in Caiden, G.E. (ed.) *International Handbook of the Ombudsman. Evolution and Present Function.* London, Greenwood Press.

Meriden (1991) *Conference Report on the United Kingdom Ombudsman Conference, 17–18 October 1991*. Meriden.

Ministry of Health (1968) *National Health Service. The Administrative Structure of the Medical and Related Services in England and Wales*. London, HMSO.

Moore, V. (1991) Some reflections of the role of the ombudsman, International Institute of Administrative Sciences Conference paper, Copenhagen.

OFT (1991) *Consumer Redress: a Report by the Director General of Fair Trading into Systems for Resolving Consumer Complaints*. London, Office of Fair Trading.

Powles, G. (1979) Special referral sections in ombudsman statutes, Occasional Paper No. 1. Edmonton, Alberta, International Ombudsman Institute.

Pugh, I. (1978) The ombudsman – jurisdiction, power and practice, *Public Administration*, 56, 127.

Rawlings, R. (1986a) Parliamentary redress of grievance, in Harlow, C. (ed.) *Public Law and Politics*. London, Sweet and Maxwell.

Rawlings, R. (1986b) *The Complaints Industry: a Review of Socio-Legal Research on Aspects of Administrative Justice*. London, ESRC.

Redcliffe-Maud (1974) *Report of the Committee on Local Government Rules of Conduct*, Cmnd 5636. London, HMSO.

Reid, W. (1992) An independent voice, *The House Magazine*, 17 (542), 5–6.

Robb, B. (1967) *Sans Everything*. London, Nelson.

Rowat, D. (1968) *The Ombudsman: Citizens Defender*. London, George Allen and Unwin.

Rowat, D. (1985) *The Ombudsman Plan*. London, University Press of America.

Royal Commission (1976) *Report of the Royal Commission on Standards of Conduct in Public Life*, Cmnd 625. London, HMSO.

SDP (1983) *Controlling the State: Towards Fairer Administration*. London, Social Democratic Party.

Serota, B. (1983) The evolution of the role of the ombudsman – comparisons and perspectives, in Caiden, G. (ed.) *International Handbook of the Ombudsman*. Edmonton, Alberta, International Ombudsman Institute.

Stacey, F. (1978) *Ombudsmen Compared*. Oxford, Clarendon Press.

Taggart, M. (1990) *Corporatisation, Privatisation and Public Law*, Legal Research Foundation Publication Number 31. Auckland, LRF.

Wheare, K. (1973) *Maladministration and Its Remedies*. London, Stevens and Sons.

White Paper (1965) *The Parliamentary Commissioner for Administration*, Cmnd 2767. London, HMSO.

White Paper (1970) *Reform of Local Government in England*, Cmnd 4276. London, HMSO.

White Paper (1985) *Non-Departmental Public Bodies*, Cmnd 9563. London, HMSO.

White Paper (1991) *The Citizen's Charter: Raising the Standard*, Cmnd 1599. London, HMSO.

Widdicombe, D. (1986) *Report of the Committee of Inquiry on the Conduct of Local Authority Business*, Cmnd 9797. London, HMSO.

Williams, D. (1976) *Maladministration: Remedies for Injustice*. London, Oyez Publishing.

Wiltshire, K. (1988) The ombudsman and the legislature, *Fourth International Ombudsman Conference Papers*, Canberra, 145.

Woolf, H. (1990) *The Protection of the Public – a New Challenge*. London, Stevens.

Yardley, D. (1983) Local ombudsmen in England: recent trends and developments, *Public Law*, 522.

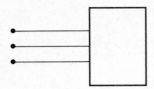

INDEX

access
    to HSC, 65, 78
    to LGO, 109–11
    to ombudsmen, 6, 14, 122, 126–7
    to PCA, 45–8, 51–3, 56, 57
ad hoc inquiries, 111
administrative review commission, 130
advisory commissioners, 117
Audit Commission, 49, 112, 129
Australian ombudsman, 45, 52, 90,
    102, 119
    own-initiative investigations, 49, 111
Austrian ombudsman, 49, 52

'bad rule', 28–9
banking ombudsman, 4, 6, 129
Barlow Clowes case, 33, 34, 48, 50,
    51, 122
building societies ombudsman, 4, 129

Citizen's Charter, 54–6, 80, 101,
    130–1
clinical complaints procedure, 62
clinical judgement, 61–3, 67, 76–7, 78

commercial matters
    see jurisdiction
complaints
    against government departments,
      40–2, 45, 50
    against hospitals, 59–60, 75–7, 81
    against local authorities, 106–7
    rejected, 36, 40, 73, 104, 106
complaints procedures
    government departments, 54, 56
    health service, 62, 70, 73, 78, 81
    local authorities, 96, 102, 103, 118
Comptroller and Auditor General, 18,
    38, 48
Council on Tribunals, 13, 64, 130
councillors, 10–11, 83, 109–10
Court Line case, 33–4
Crossman catalogue, 29

Danish ombudsman, 2, 8, 40, 52, 111
delay
    in court proceedings, 9
    in government departments, 30, 32,
      41, 42, 53

in health authorities, 67, 76, 77
in local authorities, 88, 90, 91,
    95–7, 107
and maladministration, 7, 29, 30
in ombudsman's procedures, 15, 38,
    68, 72, 73, 100
discretion to investigate, 26–7, 36, 66,
    94–5

European Community Ombudsman, 4
European Ombudsman Institute, 5
ex gratia payments
    see remedies
expenses incurred in bringing
    complaints, 37, 74, 103
exclusions of jurisdiction
    see jurisdiction

Finnish ombudsman, 2
Franks Committee, 17–18
French Mediateur, 47, 51, 52, 90,
    115, 125
further reports, 98, 99, 100, 101

good administrative practice, 81,
    115–19, 128–30
    codes, 57–8, 117, 119, 129

improving administration, 12–13,
    15–16, 129
    and PCA, 31, 57, 58
    and LGO, 115, 120
independent professional reviews, 62,
    66, 76–7
informal settlements, 12, 15, 73, 116
initiating complaints, 48–50, 71–2,
    102
injustice, 31–2, 66–8, 97–8
insurance ombudsman, 4
investigation process, 36–9, 73, 103–4
International Ombudsman Institute, 5

judicial enforcement, 35, 99, 100, 101
judicial review, 9, 64, 94, 95
jurisdiction, 16, 125
    of HSC
        generally, 61–6

commercial matters, 65
personnel matters, 64–5
s.84 inquiries, 65–6
service committees, 63–4
of LGO
    generally, 86–94
    commercial matters, 88–90
    internal educational matters, 90–3
    personnel matters, 90
    Schedule 5 exclusions, 87–93
of PCA
    generally, 19–26
    commercial matters, 23–4
    personnel matters, 24–5
    Schedule 3 exclusions, 21–6

lay adjudicators, 55
Legal Aid, 9
legal remedies, 8–9, 26–7, 66, 94–5

Maastricht Treaty, 4
maladministration, 27–31, 66–8, 95–7
    in government departments, 40–2
    in health authorities, 76–7
    in local authorities, 107
    meaning of, 7–8, 124
    see also delay
Medical Protection Society, 73–4
MPs, 15, 25, 34, 37
    grievance redress, 10–11, 21
    complaint referral, 46, 47

National Audit Office, 49
New Zealand ombudsman, 3, 6, 19
    jurisdiction, 8, 30
    numbers of cases, 50
    own-initiative investigations, 49
    staffing levels, 40
NHS Trust hospitals, 61, 74–5
non-departmental bodies, 19, 20, 54
Northern Ireland ombudsman, 1, 6,
    39, 84, 99, 108
Norwegian ombudsman, 3, 8, 115

objectives of LGO, 85
own-initiative investigations, 4, 13, 48,
    72, 111–13

Patient's Charter, 78, 80
personnel matters
   see jurisdiction
Police Complaints Authority, 1, 21, 25
prisons ombudsman, 1, 43
private sector ombudsmen, 3, 4, 5, 6,
   121, 129
publicity, 14–15, 16
   HSC, 79–81
   LGO, 113–14
   PCA, 39, 47, 50–3, 57

reasons for decisions, 89, 95–6, 119,
   129, 130
record keeping, 37, 69, 76, 95
remedies, 14, 127–8
   and HSC
      generally, 68–71
      ex gratia payments, 68
      financial, 68
      review of procedures, 69–70
   and LGO
      generally, 97–101
      compensation, 98
      review of procedures, 98
   and PCA
      generally, 32–5
      apology, 33
      ex gratia payments, 32, 33
      review of procedures, 33
Representative Body, 92, 93, 114–15

Sachsenhausen case, 33, 51
Scottish local ombudsman, 1, 6, 84

screening process for complaints,
   35–6, 72–3, 102, 104
Select Committee on the PCA
   Citizen's Charter, 55–6, 80, 130–1
   HSC, 63, 64, 68, 76–9
   LGO, 115
   member filter, 47
   non-compliance, 34, 70, 98–100
   recommendations on jurisdiction,
      23–5, 41, 49, 60, 71
   role, 53–4
single ombudsman system, 132
staffing, 44–5, 108
Swedish ombudsman, 2, 119, 121
   jurisdiction, 49, 115
   numbers of cases, 40, 50
   own-initiative investigations, 111

time limit for complaints, 27, 36,
   71–2, 95
time taken to investigate, 38, 74, 105
tribunals, 10, 18, 27, 123, 124
   appeals, 26, 36, 66, 94
   ombudsman's jurisdiction, 20, 22–3
two-tier investigations, 39

UK Ombudsman Association, 6, 132

Welsh local ombudsman, 1, 6, 84
Whyatt Committee, 7, 17
   function of ombudsman, 13, 18, 27,
      57, 124
   member filter, 45, 46
   terms of reference, 18